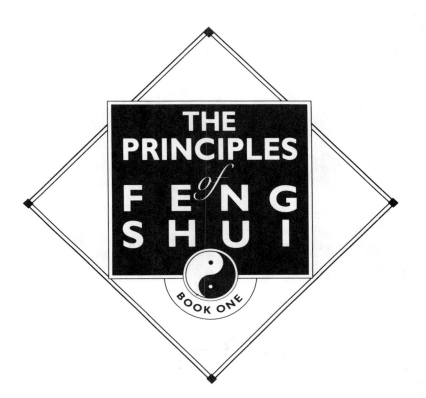

THE PRINCIPLES of FENG SHUI

BOOK ONE

D1366676

Published by The American Feng Shui Institute.
108 North Ynez Avenue, Suite 202
Monterey Park, California 91754

First Published January 1995
Second Edition November 1996
Third Edition April 1999

Writer: Master Larry Sang
Co-Writer & Translator: Helen Luk
Design & Illustrations: Jason Lam
Cover Design: Jason Lam
Revision Edit: Jessie Cho

ISBN 0-9644583-0-6

5 1 8 7 5

9 780964 458307

Disclaimer

This book   presents information and techniques that have been in use throughout the Orient for many years. The information offered is to the author's best knowledge and experiences and makes no claims for absolute effectiveness. It can be beneficial or harmful, depending upon one's stage of development. Readers should use their own discretion and liability. The adoption and application of the material offered in this book is solely the reader's own responsibility. The authors and publisher of this book are not responsible or liable in any manner for loss or damage of properties or bodily injuries that may occur through following the instructions in this book.

THE AMERICAN FENG SHUI INSTITUTE

The American Feng Shui Institute was established in California in 1991.

Master Larry Sang, the founder, has brought this traditional knowledge to the West with the following objectives in mind: They are to:

•   Introduce the ancient knowledge of Feng Shui to the interested public.

•   Provide Students with the proper theories and techniques of Feng Shui.

•   Offer students opportunities to become professional Feng Shui Practitioners.

•   Guarantee that these practitioners are professionally trained to extend proper guidance to those seeking assistance.

•   Ensure that students who are interested in teaching Feng Shui are properly trained.

For more information, please write to:

American Feng Shui Institute
108 North Ynez Avenue, Suite 202
Monterey Park, California 91754

Individuals interested in being on our mailing list for Feng Shui seminars, Chinese astrology, palm and face reading, etc., should complete the application form at the end of this book and mail it to the above address.

As a practicing architect and developer who has been involved in real estate development for the past twenty years in Southern California, I have always been amazed by the amount of interest in the practice of *"Feng Shui"* Most of the projects that I have involved in required some degree of *"Feng Shui "* reading either in the planning stage of the project or after the project is completed before occupancy. In many cases, this additional criteria of *"good Feng Shui"* becomes one of the determining factor of the project's success or failure.

Even though this ancient knowledge has become a popular subject and has been used widely in Asia, there are not too many organized books or documentation to clearly explain the principal theory of *"Feng Shui"*. Most of the documentation was in ancient Chinese books that required a very good understanding of Chinese culture and literature or a long term personal instruction from a *"Feng Shui"* master in order to acquire this knowledge. I feel extremely fortunate to have met Master Sang about ten years ago and started to learn the principal and theory of *"Feng Shui"* to improve my practice of architecture and real estate development projects. I am particularly please to know that Master Sang has finally decided to compile his teaching material into a book form. This book will benefit the modern "Feng Shui" practitioners so more people can learn from this knowledge of controlling and balancing the surroundings to achieve happiness, prosperity and health.

Learning the rules of *"Feng Shui"* from Master Sang. It is very much like learning the basic theory of architectural and environmental design. It involves the correct placement of architectural elements, dealing with the surrounding environment, orientation of building, circulations, color, room shape and location to create a comfortable and balanced environment. It is logical and scientific. It should not be mistakenly affiliated with superstitions or religions.

I congratulate Master Sang and solute to his contributions to the art of *"Feng Shui"*. I wish this ancient knowledge can be expanded and utilized correctly by the users of this book to benefit the health, happiness and prosperity of mankind.

Raymond Cheng AIA, NCARB
President of California State Board of Architectural Examiner 1997

About The Authors

Dr. Larry Sang is the foremost authority on Feng Shui in the United States. Raised in Hong Kong, Dr. Sang began practicing Feng Shui almost 25 years ago and had hosted Feng Shui and Astrology programs in the Southern California Chinese Broadcasting Radio.

Dr. Sang has taught seminars jointly sponsored by the University of Southern California and The Northrop University as well as classes at the Samra University of Oriental Medicine. In 1991, Master Sang established The American Feng Shui Institute and the American Society of Feng Shui. Since its inception, the Institute has recruited hundreds of students from all walks of life. Master Sang presently is compiling material for his upcoming books. The next is entitled *The Environment of Feng Shui – Book II.*

Helen Luk is an instructor of the American Feng Shui Institute. She has been studying Yi-Jing with Master Sang and for years has been a devotee of various kinds of Chinese astrology.

ACKNOWLEDGMENTS

First, I thank the students of the American Feng Shui Institute for conceiving **The Principles of Feng Shui.** They diligently urged me to compile and revise years of teaching materials into this book that serves as an introduction of orthodox Feng Shui.

I thank my student, Helen Luk, for contributing her fluent translations, outstanding editing and organizational skills to this book. Special thanks go to Jason Lam for his professional and elegant illustrations that add substantial comprehension to my work.

As always, I am grateful to my wife, Salina, for her unlimited support and understanding in bringing this book to being. Otherwise, my freedom-loving nature and lack of a disciplined work routine would not have allowed me to produce this kind of systematic writing without her constant encouragement.

Finally, I wish to extend sincere thanks to numerous friends and acquaintances who offered valuable comments and suggestions that enabled **The Principles of Feng Shui** to come into publication.

ACKNOWLEDGMENTS

Translating and co-writing this book has been a whole new experience for me. For someone who has no prior writing training, this task has been particularly challenging. The long hours sitting in front of the computer with wide and dried eyes trying to figure out the right word or to master the PageMaker have both been fun and at times frustrating. I could not have pulled this through without the help and support from the following friends:

My gratefulness to "Si Fu" (Master Sang) for giving me the opportunity to participate in this wonderful project. My sincerest thanks to him for his trust, support and his kindness in teaching me more than I could ask for.

My thanks to a good friend, Julia, for her patience in editing for me. Without her, this book can never be published.

Many thanks to Jason, my best friend, for his generosity in lending me his illustrations (which are to also appear in Book II, The Environment of Feng Shui) and his kind words of support when needed. Also much thanks for his technical and production assistance which I cannot do without.

Thanks to relatives and friends who know of this book-writing idea and have kept the laughs to themselves.

Last but not least, my first copy of this book is going out to a great lady who knows only of giving. Thank you, Mom, for all.

Helen Luk
Califorma
September 1994

TABLE OF CONTENTS

Chapter One — AN OVERVIEW OF FENG SHUI 1
Feng Shui 2
The History 3
Why Feng Shui Remained Obscure in Ancient China 4
Feng Shui Today 5
The Basics 6

Chapter Two — THE YIN YANG PRINCIPLE 7
Yin/Yang — The Two Primal Energies 8

Chapter Three — THE FIVE ELEMENTS 13
More on The Yin/Yang Principle 15
What are The Five Elements 17
The Productive Cycle 19
The Domination Cycle 20
The Reductive Cycle 21
The Five Elements and Their Correspondences 22
    (Table 3.1)
Usage of The Five Elements 23
Remedies 24

Chapter Four — THE EIGHT TRIGRAMS 31
The Ba Gua (The Eight Trigrams) 32
    Kun 33
    Chen 34
    Kan 35
    Ken 36
    Chien 37
    Sun 38
    Li 39
    Tui 40
The Eight Trigram Grid 41
Practical Experience 42

Chapter Five — THE DIRECTIONS (East/West System)   45
Essential Directives to Practicing Feng Shui   46
   The East/West System   46
      A. Personal Trigram   46
      B. House Trigram   47
   How to Determine a Personal Trigram   47
   More on Finding a Personal Trigram   48
   Personal Trigram Formulas   49
      A. Males   49
      B. Females   50
   Personal Trigram Chart   52
   How to Determine a House Trigram   54
   The Directions   54
   Finding Sitting and Facing Directions of Buildings 59
   Practical Skills — Use of a Lo Pan   61
      A. Parts of Sang's Lo Pan   64
      B. Proper Procedures on Using Sang's Lo Pan 66
      C. Care of a Lo Pan   68
   Matching a Personal Trigram with a House Trigram   68
   The Eight Trigrams (Ba Gua) Letter System   77
      A. Rules and Guidelines to Transform the Eight
         Trigrams (Personal and House)   80
      B. Symbologies of the Eight Trigram Letter
         System   90
      C. More Examples of Transformation 91
      D. East Group   94
      E. West Group   96
   Putting the East/West System to Work   98
   More on the Personal/House Trigram Match   102
Spousal Personal Trigram and House Trigram Match   105
Entrances   108
Bedrooms   111

Other Concerns of a Bedroom   113
Colors of The Five Elements — The Productive Cycle   123
Colors of The Five Elements — The Domination Cycle   124
Colors of The Five Elements — The Reductive Cycle   125
Kitchen and Stove   126

Chapter Six — THE XUAN KONG SYSTEM   131
The Xuan Kong System   132
What is Xuan Kong   132
More about Xuan Kong   133
  A. The Solar System and Its Influences on Us   133
  B. Xuan Kong System AKA Zi-Bai Fu   134
The Floating   138
Quick Reference Guide   152
The Second Number — The Annual Number   154
The Annual Number Chart   157
Combining the Two Numbers   158
How to Analyze   159

Chapter Seven — THE ENVIRONMENT   173

Chapter Eight — QUESTIONS AND ANSWERS   193

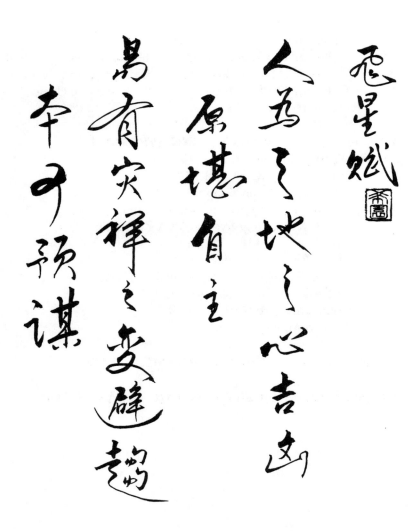

Calligraphy by Larry Sang

"Since Man is the heart of the universe, he should be able to determine his own fate."
"Since change involves fortune and misfortune, its outcome should be predictable."

Foreword

Feng Shui, a Chinese mathematical system developed by scholars through observations accumulated over thousands of years, is a method of harmonizing a man-made environment and the calculation of time and space. It is a science incorporatiang astronomy, geography, the environment, the magnetic fields, and physics. Contrary to popular belief, Feng Shui is not a religion or superstition. Modern science has proven it to be a complex mathematical system.

The two systems discussed in this book are excerpt from two Feng Shui classics:

" Ba Zhai Mirror " (八宅明鏡) and
" Shen's Xuan Kong Teaching " (沈氏玄空)

Feng Shui is gradually gaining recognition in the West, due partly to a society that is more conscious of the needs of our natural and artificial environments. Unfortunately, this recent resurgence of practicing Feng Shui also has generated misconception and misuses. There are those barely knowledgeable in the basics who are manipulating the growing popularity of Feng Shui. An accomplished Feng Shui master acquires his expertise through years of study, apprenticeship and practice. With this book, I hope to enlighten you to the proper usage of Feng Shui, as well as to legitimize its practicality and value in today's modern society.

For novices as well as for the initiated, this book is an indispensable guide toFeng Shui theories. It progresses from the basic Eight Trigrams to more advanced mathematical analyses. I have also included, where relevant, personal experienced to illustrate how a theory can be applied.

This book will enhance your awareness of the law and order of the universe and the power of nature, yet you also will be empowered with the knowledge to manipulate your surroundings so as to affect your finances, health, and emotions.

This book has been revised to use the Pinyin system of transliteration. Pinyin has become the standard method of writing the sound of Mandarin Chinese words into our alphabet. "Ch'i" becomes "qi." "Taoism" become "Daoism"

The only words in the book that we did not change to Pinyin were the names of the eight trigrams and the lo pan (Chinese Feng Shui compass). We could not do this because then the spelling would not match the spelling on the lo pan. This would cause confusion for people learning Feng Shui from the book.

Below is a table with these words, as found in the book, and the pinyin spelling:

Spelling in book	Pinyin
Lo pan	Luo pan
Kan	Kan
Kun	Kun
Chen	Zhen
Sun	Sun
Chien	Qian
Tui	Dui
Ken	Gen
Li	Li

AN OVERVIEW OF FENG SHUI

FENG SHUI

"Kan Yu," meaning "Raise the head and observe the sky above. Lower the head and observe the environment around us," is an ancient term for Feng Shui. Feng Shui is a natural science which theorizes that the environment is considered an integral element in the art of living. Feng Shui literally means Wind and Water. In the western world, it is most often known as Chinese Geomancy.

Based on the interactions among the movements of the orbiting planets of the solar system (heaven), living environment (earth), and one's birth date (individual), Feng Shui is a unique system that mathematically devises the most favorable direction for one's living quarter and work place. Evolved through thousands of years of unrelinquished experiments and observations of the world's orderliness, Feng Shui has proven to be a sound and complete system.

氣： 乘風則散
界水則止

"Qi", disperse while riding with the **WIND**,
stall when reaching the edge of **WATER**.

"All beings in this universe are governed by the laws of nature" is an undisputable axiom. Qi plays an important role in Feng Shui; it is the energy, current, or magnetic fields in nature. In our body, Qi serves as the air we breathe. It is a mechanism of life and a vital force. To identify, and at the same time, use Qi is an important Feng Shui concept. Qi, directed in an appropriate way in our environment, enhances career advancement, brings prosperity, and ensures health.

Recognizing that time, space, and weather imposes adverse influence and creates imbalance in all living things, ancient Feng Shui scholars and practitioners developed formulas to counteract such forces of nature by combining the Qi concept with the Yin/Yang theory, the Five Elements (Metal, Water, Wood, Fire, Earth) and its "productive" and "domination" cycles. Chemical reactions among the Five Elements, as well as the interactions between Qi and Time and Space, are known to have direct and indirect effects on life. Effects may be obvious or discreet.

The planets govern time and movement that affect nature and all life on earth. For instance, people who live near mountains have different personalities than those who live by the sea. People living near mountains are mostly compassionate and kind, but rather stubborn; while those by the sea are generally more intelligent, adaptive, and agile. Residents of homes built near electromagnetic plants are now believed to have a higher possibility of developing malignant diseases. Current reports state how different magnetic fields can affect one's genes, neural system, and heredity. These are the scientific fundamentals of Feng Shui.

THE HISTORY

Feng Shui has a history of over two thousand years. As early as 25 A.D., during the East Han Dynasty, manuals and literature on the teaching of Feng Shui have been found. During the Early Spring and Warring State (770 B.C.- 475 B.C.), the Yin/Yang theory was at its peak of popularity. Feng Shui, primarily based on the Yin/Yang theory, is believed to have been developed during that same period.

Of the many respectable scholars and practitioners who have contributed to the establishment of Feng Shui, the four most prominent were from the

Of the many respectable scholars and practitioners who have contributed to the establishment of Feng Shui, the four most prominent were from the Tang and Song dynasties:

YANG Yun-Song	楊 均 松
ZENG Wen-Shan	曾 文 汕
LIAO Yu	廖　瑀
LAI Ren-Wen	賴 俊 文

Yang, in particular, is most revered by today's practitioners.

During the Yellow Bandits Rebellion (907 A.D.), Yang, an astronomer and the emperor's meteorologist, fled the Imperial Palace with some valuable and irreplaceable collections on Feng Shui. He hid in anonymity in the mountainous northwest region of Jiang Xi Province (江 西 省) and helped many, especially the poor, by using his knowledge in Feng Shui. He renamed himself as Save The Poor (楊 救 貧) and is remembered not only for his accomplishments but also for his having made known to the commoners the long-kept secret of Feng Shui.

WHY FENG SHUI REMAINED OBSCURE IN ANCIENT CHINA

Feng Shui applies both to a Yin house and a Yang house. A Yin house means "dwelling for the deceased", while a Yang house means "shelter for the living". In Feng Shui, a desirable burial site is a guarantee of prosperity, fortune, and power for one's descendants. The same applies to a Yang house that is deemed Wang Shan Wang Shui (good for money, good for people).

In ancient China, emperors, nobles, and the privileged few deliberately kept Feng Shui to themselves to secure their thrones. All literature about Feng Shui was forbidden to commoners. Literature would be confiscated if found in their possession. Expert practitioners of Feng Shui served the elite exclusively and were generously rewarded.

However, dissenters were severely punished or even killed. Therefore, Feng Shui was available to the privileged few and commoners remained ignorant of its existence. Since Feng Shui was a closely guarded secret, its divulgence and the impartation of its techniques were treated with reverence. As with a family profession, it was passed through generations within a family.

Though it was possible for an outsider to have been selected as an apprentice, he had to meet stringent criteria. Once chosen, apprenticeship meant persistence, humility and lifetime devotion. Most of the teaching was done verbally, as the subject was too confidential for print. Theories were manifested in the form of poems that students had to learn by rote.

FENG SHUI TODAY

Since its inception, interest in Feng Shui has never dwindled. Immense interest is now growing in Australia, the United States, and Canada, due largely to the number of Chinese immigrating to these countries.

Feng Shui has always fascinated the Chinese. Many have heard folklore on how Feng Shui has managed to save lives and bring prosperity. Ornaments, such as mirrors and wind chimes are often seen hanging on the walls or doors of many Chinese homes. One could be in an office or a house that has been refurbished according to a Feng Shui master's ideas and instructions. To many Chinese, Feng Shui is a household word and they refer to it day to day.

Because of its increasing popularity, the principles of Feng Shui have often been misinterpreted. Some claim to be experts when, in fact, they possess only a rudimentary understanding of the subject.

They distort theories by integrating elements and ideas alien to Feng Shui. Since the most visible elements of Feng Shui to some people are mirrors and wind chimes hanging in homes, the practice of it is regarded as being too simplistic to be a form of natural science; and thus Feng Shui is mistakenly affiliated with religion.

THE BASICS

Feng Shui consists of six scientific theories and principles that have endured more than two thousand years of tests and experiments. As with all sciences, a good understanding of the fundamentals is a prerequisite for those who seriously want to practice Feng Shui. The basic fundamentals are:

      1)   The Yin/Yang Principle
      2)   The Theory of Five Elements
      3)   The Eight Trigrams
      4)   The Directions (East/West System)
      5)   The Solar System (Xuan Kong System)
      6)   The Environment

THE YIN/YANG PRINCIPLE

CHAPTER 2

YIN/YANG - THE TWO PRIMAL ENERGIES

In *Yi-Jing, the Book of Change*, Yin/Yang are illustrated as two polar opposites that exist in the universe. We find ourselves living in a world of constant change and, these changes are eternal and perpetual. Change is the essence of law. The world is a place of plants, people and other beings, all oscillating from birth to death. Seasons change from the heat of summer to the cold of winter. The activities of this endless to and fro movement of change are commonly referred to as the Yin/Yang Principle: the two primal energies of the universe.

TAI   JI

Figure 2-1

YIN/YANG CORRESPONDENCES

YIN

Black
Death
Winter
Cold
Female
Passive
Night

Figure 2-2

YANG

White
Life
Summer
Hot
Male
Active
Day

Figure 2-3

Tai Ji (see Figure 2-1) is the universal symbol for the Yin/Yang principle. A circle is used to display high activities and indefinite movements. There is neither a beginning nor an end. The Yin (black) is separated from the Yang (white) by an "S" curve; this further defines that nothing is absolute. The S curve clearly illustrates:

久　動　必　靜

Lengthy Activity (Yang) is followed by Stillness (Yin).

久　靜　必　動

Prolonged Dormancy (Yin) always results in Mobility (Yang).

The S curve reflects the activities and the perpetually changing law and order of the universe, as well as the harmonious interaction between Yin and Yang forces. Imagine the heat of summer (white) as it builds up and soon peaks, giving rise to the cold of winter (black); or the constant change of day and night. The small dark circle on the Yang side and the small white circle on the Yin side, indicate BALANCE between Yin and Yang: in Yin, there is always Yang, and in Yang, there is always Yin. Each force is distinct and individual, but they are inseparable. Yin and Yang are like two sides of the same coin — one cannot exist without the other, just as without female, there can be no male. We cannot know what cold is without experiencing heat. Opposites are constantly interacting with each other. Maintaining a balance between Yin and Yang in one's body results in good health, and maintaining the same kind of balance in your living environment is the key to good Feng Shui.

The immutable laws of the universe – no matter how complicated they may seem -- collectively speaking are the interaction and the relationship between the two polar energies, Yin and Yang. Westerners may find the concept of the Chinese Yin/Yang principle vague and incomprehensible. In fact, the Yin/Yang principle can be dissected and explained by applying a scientific point of view.

What is Yin? And what is Yang? We have briefly discussed that the nature of Yin is cold and passive and that of Yang is hot and active (see figures 2-2 and 2-3). In terms of physics, Yin is the internal pulling force while Yang is the external pushing force. Yin is cold, and cold objects often possess a contracting ability. Yang is hot, and hot objects generally maintain an expanding ability. From these, we understand that the Yin/Yang principle and modern physics share the same theory.

In Feng Shui, much emphasis rests on Yin and Yang. For example, living in an excessively bright environment will cause headaches, quick temperament, and easily troubled emotions; while an environment that is too dark will result in desperation, pessimism, and fatigue. The former example has excessive Yang and the latter shows excessive Yin. Both are good examples of Yin/Yang imbalances.

Years ago, a woman residing in the mid-mountain level of Hong Kong island had an incurable headache, even after numerous medical visits. She finally sought help through Feng Shui. Through friends, she contacted me and invited me over to her house for a reading. The residence was in an upper middle-class area, located on the eleventh floor of a condominium facing the harbor. Both the living room and her bedroom shared the same spectacular view of the harbor, both rooms had picturesque windows extending from the ceiling to the floor.

From 8:00 a.m. until late afternoon, both rooms were so resplendently lit by hot sun rays that the rooms appeared to burnished.   In summertime, it was even worse, Any experienced Feng Shui practitioner could tell the source of her headache in one glance of the aprtment. I suggested that she cover the windows with darker-colored drapes to neutralize the glare from the sun and, at the same time, to put a metal alarm clock in the bedroom as a remedy for the numbers 2 and 5 (see Chapter Six, The Xuan Kong System). Other than the aforementioned problems, the residence was a desirable Wang Shan Wang Shui (good for money, good for people) house. A few days later, the woman told me that her headache was finally gone without having ever taken any medication since my visit. This is a good example of Yin/Yang imbalance with excessive Yang.

THE FIVE ELEMENTS

The Five Elements

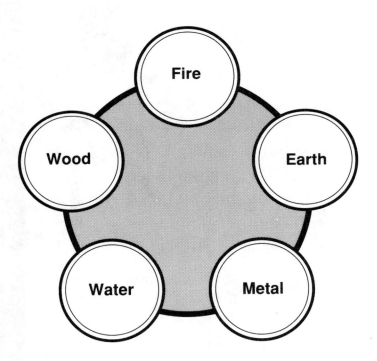

Figure 3-1

MORE ON THE YIN/YANG PRINCIPLE

Prior to discussing The Five Elements and their roles in Feng Shui, it is important for us to once again talk about the Tai Ji and the Yin/ Yang Principle. Tai Ji illustrates the overall existence of all living things. Yin/Yang is the evolution of all beings. The Five Elements are the interactions that occur during the evolutions.

TAI JI

Figure 3-2

Today's scientists, for the convenience of research and development, often separate the Yin from the Yang. This serves as an easier way to explain the development and growth of all things. In fact, to categorize everything under Yin or Yang is impossible. There are often heated arguments between scientists and philosophers over theories. Scientists favor classifying all things and all beings into different groups and categories. Their observances are usually made in a shorter span of time and space than philosophers who tend to observe natural phenomena over a longer period of time. Philosophers also take a wider perspective and hypothesize that all things are correlated.

Feng Shui was originally derived from Yi-Jing, a book containing theories based on philosophy, logic, and sientific methods. Therefore, according to the Tai Ji of Yi-Jing, in the Yin/Yang Principle, all beings, interact with each other:

同中有異　異中有同

In Similarity, there is Variation ;
And in Variation, Similarity is found.

常中有變　變中有常

In Consistency, you can find Changes;
And in Changes, there are always Consistencies.

凶中有吉　吉中有凶

Behind the screen of Misfortune, there is the presence of Fortune;
Whereas in Fortune, hidden Misfortunes await.

In conclusion, in a Yang, there is always a Yin. And in a Yin, there is always a Yang.

Using the Tai Ji figure to represent the universe, one finds the Yin/Yang principle in all things as enveloping and encompassing. There is a saying:

孤陰不生　獨陽不長

Lone Yin does not Grow
Solitary Yang does not Thrive.

For example, Left and Right coexist. Should the Left vanish, the Right is no longer valid. This clearly proves that Left is Right, and Right is Left.   Separating Yin from Yang in a Tai Ji is only a hypothesis. To only hypothesize in any science is limiting.

What   are The Five Elements

The Five Elements are manifestations of Qi and the interactions during evolutions. In all beings besides the oscillating Yin/Yang forces are other remarkable correlations. They are:

Directions: East, South, West, North, Center.
Emotions: Bliss, Anger, Sorrow, Joy, Fear
Vowels: A, E, I, O, U

To better analyze the interactions between all things, the Chinese developed the theory of The Five Elements (Wu Xing), namely Metal, Water, Wood, Fire, and Earth. All beings in this universe are influenced by the interactions of these five elements. As these interactions are systematic and disciplinary, they can be predicted and serve as the essence of the natural environment.

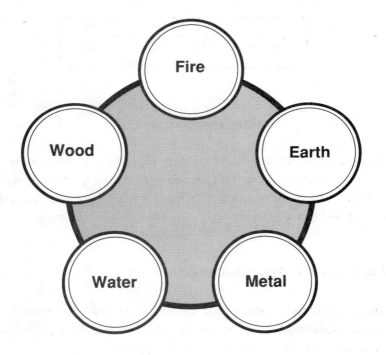

Figure 3-3

The cyclic interactions of these five elements can be employed to explain the interrelations of all substances and existences in the universe. These energy interplays are The Productive Cycle, The Domination Cycle, and The Reductive Cycle (Figures 3-4, 3-5 and 3-6 respectively).

The Productive Cycle

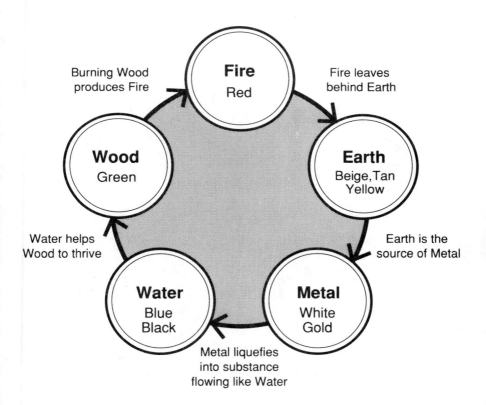

Figure 3-4

The Productive Cycle is one of balance. Each element in this cycle produces or generates the succeeding element. Burning wood produces fire. Residue from fire forms the earth. Earth is the source of metal. Metal liquefies like water. Water helps trees to thrive, supplying wood for the fire.

The Domination Cycle

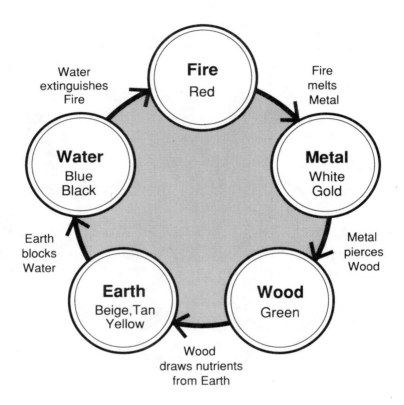

Figure 3-5

In the Domination Cycle, each element destroys the succeeding element. It is therefore considered to be a cycle of imbalance. Fire melts metal and metal pierces wood. Wood draws from the earth. Earth blocks water and finally, water extinguishes fire.

The Reductive Cycle

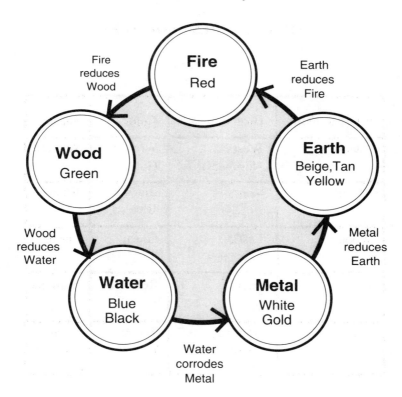

Figure 3-6

There is often little or no mention of this third cycle where the theory of The Five Elements and their cycles are discussed. The Reductive Cycle is considered significant in Feng Shui as it serves as the remedy for bad Feng Shui. It is also the means to correct the imbalances as seen in the Domination Cycle. In this cycle, earth reduces fire. Fire burns wood. Wood draws from water. Water reduces metal, and metal reduces earth. The Reduction Cycle will offset the imbalances, diminish the adversities, and lead the environment back into desirable productivity.

THE FIVE ELEMENTS
&
THEIR CORRESPONDENCES

Five Elements	Direction	Color	Season
Metal	West & Northwest	White & Gold	Autumn
Water	North	Black & Blue	Winter
Wood	East & Southeast	Green	Spring
Fire	South	Red	Summer
Earth	Northeast, Southwest & Center	Tan & Yellow	Indian Summer

Table 3.1

USAGE OF THE FIVE ELEMENTS

Correcting any dominant interaction between two elements can be achieved by either using the element itself or its corresponding color(s). However, using the actual element takes precedence over the use of the elemental color(s).

Metal
Any decorative metal ornaments or sculptures or the representative colors white and gold.

Water
Aquariums, clean moving water, or the colors blue and black.

Wood
Trees or stalks of plants, or color green.

Fire
A burning fireplace, lamps with red shades, or its corresponding color red.

Earth
Rocks, earth sculptures, clay figurines, or the colors tan and yellow.

Please note that when using the elemental color(s), you can choose to place rugs, furnishings or upholstery in areas that need correction. Objects used should only be of ONE color. Hence, pictures or tapestries with a mixture of colors and a chief main-color background will not be as effective.

REMEDIES

The elements that are shown in *Italics* are the remedies for the different domination cycles.

1)   In a situation where metal dominates (pierces) wood, water is brought in to reduce the metal and simultaneously nourish the wood. One might question that since fire dominates metal, why not use fire to melt the metal instead. Fire will certainly destroy metal, but, at the same time, it will also reduce the wood and, therefore, fire will become too dominant in this situation to elements.

Metal — *Water* — Wood

Photo 3-1

An attractive looking container that holds clean, running (moving) water is a good example of the Water element as a remedy.

2)   When water dominates fire, wood is added, since wood will reduce (draw) the water and, at the same time, helps to produce fire.

Water — *Wood* — Fire

Photo 3-2

A strong healthy potted plant is recommended. Wood furniture is dead and processed wood, and should not be considered as a remedy representing the Wood element in Feng Shui.

3)   When wood dominates earth, bring in fire to reduce the wood and to relieve the earth from the dominance of wood. The metal element is not suggested in this case because metal will dominate wood and reduce earth simultaneously.

Wood — Fire — Earth

Photo 3-3

We suggest using a lamp with a red shade (let the lamp remain on for 24 hours, when possible) or red color rug to replace the Fire element when actual fire is not feasible. Photo 3-3 shows candles that, when lit, are good examples of the Fire element.

4)   Fire dominates metal. Earth will remedy the imbalance, since it puts out fire and also produces metal.

Fire — *Earth* — Metal

Photo 3-4

Earthen-made objects, such as vases, clay pots, urns and rock sculptures are good examples of Earth element remedies.

5)   Earth blocks the flow of water. Metal will help to relieve the water from the domination of earth by reducing the earth and strengthening the water.

Earth — *Metal* — Water

Photo 3-5

Decorative metal ornaments or sculptures are often suggested as Metal element remedies. An ornament that has moving metal parts and produces constant metallic sounds, such as a grandfather clock, is most effective and preferable.

	Productive Cycle	Domination Cycle	Remedy
Water & Earth		Yes	Metal
Fire & Water		Yes	Wood
Wood & Metal		Yes	Water
Metal & Earth	Yes		N/A
Wood & Water	Yes		N/A
Fire & Wood	Yes		N/A
Water & Metal	Yes		N/A
Metal & Fire		Yes	Earth
Fire & Earth	Yes		N/A
Earth & Wood		Yes	Fire

Table 3.2

Note:

The Reductive Cycle only acts as means for remedies. The relationship between any two elements will only fall under either the Productive Cycle or the Domination Cycle.

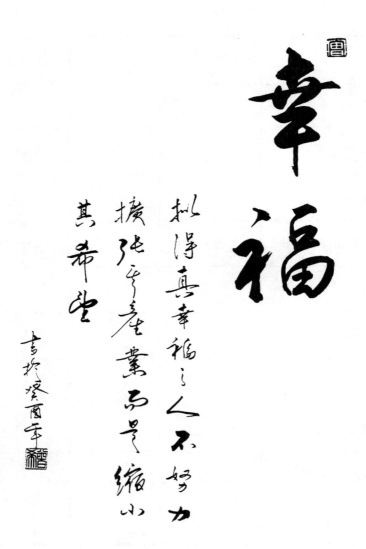

Calligraphy by Larry Sang

"In order to attain real happiness, one should not expand his assets but rather lessen his desires."

THE EIGHT TRIGRAMS

THE BA GUA (THE EIGHT TRIGRAMS)

The Tai Ji symbol is further simplified by the following figure:

Figure 4-1

Yin is represented by one broken line
Yang is represented by one straight line

Through evolutions, figure 4-1 gives rise to more complex symbols, as the Eight Trigrams 八 卦 (pronounced Ba Gua). The trigrams are read from the bottom. The lowest (or the 1st) line represents Earth. The middle (or the 2nd) line represents Man. The top (3rd) line represents Heaven. Each of the following eight trigrams is assigned on corresponding familial relation(s), direction, cosmic phenomenon, element, part(s) of body, illness(es), and number.

3rd	━━━━━━	Heaven
2nd	━━━━━━	Man
1st	━━━━━━	Earth

Kun

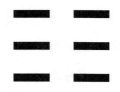

Symbology:	Earth
Familial Relations:	Mother, Wife (or old woman)
Direction:	Southwest
Element:	Earth
Elemental Color:	Tan, Yellow
Parts of Body:	Abdomen, Stomach
Illnesses:	Digestive or Reproductive Disorders
Number:	2

Chen

Symbology:	Thunder
Familial Relations:	Eldest Son
Direction:	East
Element:	Hard Wood
Elemental Color:	Green
Parts of Body:	Feet, Throat
Illnesses:	Hysteria, Convulsions, etc.
Number:	3

Kan

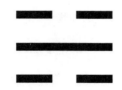

Symbology:	Water
Familial Relations:	Middle Son (or middle-aged man)
Direction:	North
Element:	Water
Elemental Color:	Blue, Black
Parts of Body:	Ears, Blood, Kidneys
Illnesses:	Earache, Kidney Ailments
Number:	1

Ken

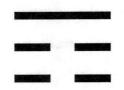

Symbology:	Mountain
Familial Relations:	Youngest Son (or youth)
Direction:	Northeast
Element:	Earth
Elemental Color:	Tan, Yellow
Parts of Body:	Hands and Fingers
Illnesses:	Arthritis, Broken Hands
Number:	8

Chien

Symbology: Heaven
Familial Relations: Father, Husband, Owner, President
Direction: Northwest
Element: Hard Metal
Elemental Color: Gold
Parts of Body: Head and Lungs
Illnesses: Headaches, Pulmonary Diseases
Number: 6

Sun

Symbology:	Wind
Familial Relations:	Eldest Daughter, Traveller
Direction:	Southeast
Element:	Soft Wood
Elemental Color:	Green
Parts of Body:	Thighs and Buttocks
Illnesses:	Colds and Rheumatism
Number:	4

Li

Symbology:	Fire
Familial Relations:	Second Daughter (or middle-aged woman)
Direction:	South
Element:	Fire
Elemental Color:	Red
Parts of Body:	Eyes and Heart
Illnesses:	Eyes, Heart and related diseases
Number:	9

Tui

Symbology:	Marsh
Familial Relations:	Youngest Daughter (or young girl)
Direction:	West
Element:	Soft Metal
Elemental Color:	Gold
Parts of Body:	Mouth, Chest and Teeth
Illnesses:	Mouth – and Chest-related diseases
Number:	7

The Eight Trigram (Ba Gua) Grid

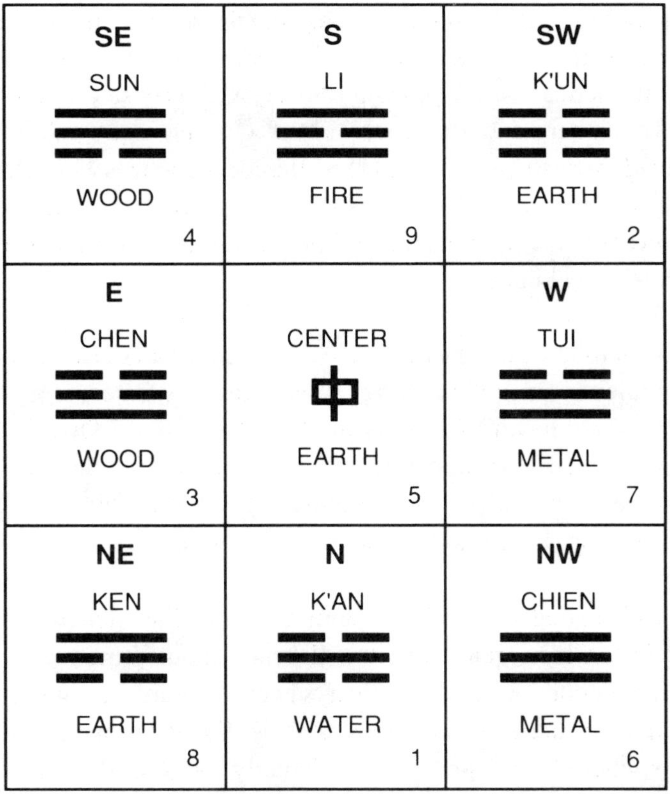

SE SUN WOOD 4	S LI FIRE 9	SW K'UN EARTH 2
E CHEN WOOD 3	CENTER 中 EARTH 5	**W** TUI METAL 7
NE KEN EARTH 8	**N** K'AN WATER 1	**NW** CHIEN METAL 6

Figure 4-2

PRACTICAL EXPERIENCE

To be a Feng Shui practitioner, one must know by heart all information related to the Eight Trigrams.

In 1986, I was invited to a Southern California restaurant in Chinatown to do a reading. After a quick look around the restaurant, I pointed out that the direction of some stoves in the kitchen was a serious mistake. I advised that it was best to avoid using those stoves or consider repositioning them. The owner wanted to know what the consequences would be if they continued to use the stoves. I told him the consequences would be grave and particularly harmful to the restaurant's owner. Later, I learned that the owner was found in the attic of the restaurant during a fire and had died from severe burns.

The positioning of the stoves of that restaurant had defied one of the serious rules of Feng Shui: "Fire Burns Heaven's Gate"(火燒天門). What does that mean? Chien symbolizes Heaven and Owner, and its element is Metal. Fire dominates Metal. The fire used in a restaurant kitchen is on going and particularly intense. Fire burns Chien's metal, and therefore, causes harm to the owner of the premises.

Those with a good grasp of Feng Shui know that if a kitchen or stove is placed in a Chien quadrant, it will bring about rambunctious and disobedient children. This has always been accurate through my years of practice. If the Zi-Bai system (紫白飛星) results are added to the analysis where both 2 and 5 coincidentally lodge in the same Chien quadrant, this house is considered to be harmful to the owners of the house.

As previously mentioned, in order to put Feng Shui into proper practice, one must learn by heart all information related to the Eight Trigrams: their correspondences, their directions, what they symbolize, and the interactions of each of the cycles of the Five Elements. This example of the Chien trigram demonstrates the significance of all the information we have discussed or will discuss in later chapters.

Painted by Larry Sang, 1990

THE DIRECTIONS (EAST/WEST SYSTEM)

CHAPTER 5

ESSENTIAL DIRECTIVES TO PRACTICING FENG SHUI

For beginners, practicing Feng Shui requires a thorough understanding of the East/West System. The East/West System involves eight types of magnetic fields or Qi. These eight types of Qi are determined by the Eight House Trigrams, or most often known in Chinese as "Ba Zhai" (八宅). Through this system, we see how the same house may have dissimilar effects on different people. Why do I sleep better when facing west rather than east? Why do I find myself more comfortable in the next bedroom? And there are many more questions that need to be answered through this personalized system. We will also discuss the important role that Direction plays in Feng Shui.

The East/West System

B.   Personal Trigram

In the theory of Feng Shui, since all of us are born in different years, we are assigned with different properties and have directions that are favorable or unfavorable to us. Those born in the same year are further classified by male or female. By using a special formula, an individual, based on birth year and gender, is assigned to one of the Eight Trigrams. This Trigram is called the *Personal Trigram.*

The eight Personal Trigrams are also classified into both East and West groups. The four trigrams — Kan, Chen, Sun, and Li belong to the East group; whereas, the rest of the Trigrams — Chien, Kun, Tui and Ken belong to the West group. If the birth year shows that an individual belongs to one of the four Personal Trigrams in the East group, it is called East group or "East Four Ming" (東四命). If the birth year determines that one belongs to a Personal Trigram in the West group, it is also called "West Four Ming (西 四 命).

B.   House Trigram

A House Trigram is decided by the "sitting" direction of a house or building. As with the Personal Trigrams, the Eight House Trigrams are also divided into the same East and West groups. A Personal Trigram and House Trigram must match to achieve a state of harmony that leads to good fortune and health. Conversely, a mismatch leads to misfortune, poor health, financial difficulties, accidents, or bad relationships, to name a few. To summarize, an East group person living in an East group house or a West group person residing in a West group house is desirable. However, an East group person in a West group house, or a West group person in an East group house, is disagreeable and not recommended.

<u>Personal/House Trigrams</u>

East Group: Kan, Chen, Sun, and Li
West Group: Chien, Kun, Tui, and Ken

How to Determine a Personal Trigram

A Personal Trigram is primarily based on an individual's birth year. Two individuals born in the same year generally share the same Personal Trigram. We should always be aware of the gender of an individual as this will result in a different Personal Trigram. A man who was born in 1964 has a different Personal Trigram from a woman who was born in the same year.

Example 5-1:

1)   A male born on May 5, 1964, belongs to a Li trigram.
2)   A female born on May 5, 1964, belongs to a CHIEN
      trigram.

More on Finding a Personal Trigram

Another technicality with which to be concerned is February 4th or 5th on a western calendar, as it is the cut off day of a Chinese solar calendar year. Any person born before February 4th or 5th of any year must use the year prior to the actual birth year as the basis for determining the Personal Trigram. For example, if one is born on February 2, 1964, the year 1964 would be replaced with the year 1963 and then be applied to the Personal Trigram formula.

The reason is because Feng Shui is structured on the Chinese solar calendar. "Spring Establishment" (立 春) is the official first day of a Chinese new year, and falls only on the 4th or 5th of February every year of a western calendar and does not exceed this two-day period. The first day of Month One (正 月) of the Chinese lunar calendar is frequently and widely mistaken as the official day of the beginning of a Chinese new year. For readers who do not have access to a Ten Thousand-Year Calendar (萬 年 歷), a book that converts a Chinese calendar into a western calendar, or information that tells whether Feb 4th or 5th is the cut-off day for a particular year, students at our Institute often use February 5th as the cut-off day of any new Chinese calendar year.

Personal Trigram Formulas

A.   Males

Add up the four digits (xxxx) of the birth year. Then divide the sum (X) by 9. Subtract the remainder (Y) from 11. The resulting number (Z) determines the Personal Trigram.

NOTE:
1)   Should the remainder (Y) be 0, treat the remainder 0 as 9.
2)   Should the resulting number (Z) be 5, a male would belong to the KUN trigram.

Example 5-2:

Male born May 4th of xxxx

x+x+x+x	= X
X divided by 9	= ( ), remaining Y
11 - Y	= Z

Z determines the Personal Trigram

Example 5-3:

Male born May 4th of 1940

1+9+4+0	= 14
14 divided by 9	= 1, remaining 5
11 - 5	= 6

6 is the Chien trigram (see Chapter Four on The Eight Trigrams).

Example 5-4:

Male born January 3rd of 1940

1+9+3+9	= 22
22 divided by 9	= 2, remaining 4
11 - 4	= 7

7 is the Tui trigram.

B.   Females

Add up the 4 digits (xxxx) of the birth year. Divide the sum (X) by 9. Add 4 to the remainder (Y). The resulting number (Z) determines the Personal Trigram.

Note:
1) Should the remainder (Y) is 0, treat the remainder 0 as 9.
2) Use the resulting number (Z) to subtract 9 if the resulting number (Z) is larger than 9.
3) Should the resulting number (Z) be 5, a female would belong to a KEN trigram.

Example 5-5:

Female born on August 13th of xxxx

x+x+x+x	= X
X divided by 9	= ( ), remaining Y
Y + 4	= Z

Z determines the Personal Trigram.

Example 5-6:

Female born on August 13th of 1951

1+9+5+1	=	16
16 divided by 9	=	1, remaining 7
7 + 4	=	11
11 - 9	=	2

2 is the Kun trigram.

Example 5-7:

Female born on February 4th of 1951

1+9+5+0	=	15
15 divided by 9	=	1, remaining 6
6 + 4	=	10
10-9	=	1

1 is the Kan trigram.

For your convenience, we have included a Quick Reference Personal Trigram Chart on the following two pages. The chart contains Personal Trigrams for both males and females born between 1900 to 1999.

Personal Trigram Chart

Year	Trigram		Year	Trigram	
	Male	Female		Male	Female
1900	Kan	Ken	1931	Chien	Li
1901	Li	Chien	1932	Kun	Kan
1902	Ken	Tui	1933	Sun	Kun
1903	Tui	Ken	1934	Chen	Chen
1904	Chien	Li	1935	Kun	Sun
1905	Kun	Kan	1936	Kan	Ken
1906	Sun	Kun	1937	Li	Chien
1907	Chen	Chen	1938	Ken	Tui
1908	Kun	Sun	1939	Tui	Ken
1909	Kan	Ken	1940	Chien	Li
1910	Li	Chien			
			1941	Kun	Kan
1911	Ken	Tui	1942	Sun	Kun
1912	Tui	Ken	1943	Chen	Chen
1913	Chien	Li	1944	Kun	Sun
1914	Kun	Kan	1945	Kan	Ken
1915	Sun	Kun	1946	Li	Chien
1916	Chen	Chen	1947	Ken	Tui
1917	Kun	Sun	1948	Tui	Ken
1918	Kan	Ken	1949	Chien	Li
1919	Li	Chien	1950	Kun	Kan
1920	Ken	Tui			
			1951	Sun	Kun
1921	Tui	Ken	1952	Chen	Chen
1922	Chien	Li	1953	Kun	Sun
1923	Kun	Kan	1954	Kan	Ken
1924	Sun	Kun	1955	Li	Chien
1925	Chen	Chen	1956	Ken	Tui
1926	Kun	Sun	1957	Tui	Ken
1927	Kan	Ken	1958	Chien	Li
1928	Li	Chien	1959	Kun	Kan
1929	Ken	Tui	1960	Sun	Kun
1930	Tui	Ken			

Personal Trigram Chart

Year	Trigram		Year	Trigram	
	Male	Female		Male	Female
1961	Chen	Chen	1981	Kan	Ken
1962	Kun	Sun	1982	Li	Chien
1963	Kan	Ken	1983	Ken	Tui
1964	Li	Chien	1984	Tui	Ken
1965	Ken	Tui	1985	Chien	Li
1966	Tui	Ken	1986	Kun	Kan
1967	Chien	Li	1987	Sun	Kun
1968	Kun	Kan	1988	Chen	Chen
1969	Sun	Kun	1989	Kun	Sun
1970	Chen	Chen	1990	Kan	Ken
1971	Kun	Sun	1991	Li	Chien
1972	Kan	Ken	1992	Ken	Tui
1973	Li	Chien	1993	Tui	Ken
1974	Ken	Tui	1994	Chien	Li
1975	Tui	Ken	1995	Kun	Kan
1976	Chien	Li	1996	Sun	Kun
1977	Kun	Kan	1997	Chen	Chen
1978	Sun	Kun	1998	Kun	Sun
1979	Chen	Chen	1999	Kan	Ken
1980	Kun	Sun	2000	Li	Chien
			2001	Ken	Tui

Note: February 5th is the cutoff day of a new Chinese calendar year.

HOW TO DETERMINE A HOUSE TRIGRAM

The Directions

A House Trigram is solely determined by the "Sitting" direction of a building and is named after the trigram the sitting direction represents. The Sitting and Facing directions MUST be across from each other on a same bearing.

For example, in Figure 5-1, a house with a north sitting direction has a south facing direction. This house has a House Trigram of Kan, as Kan represents the direction North.

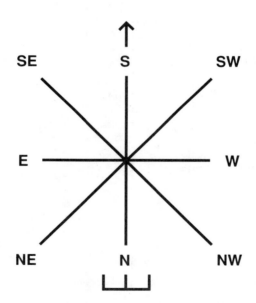

Figure 5-1

Figure 5-2 is an example of a Kun House Trigram, with a southwest sitting direction and a northeast facing direction.

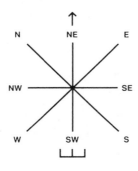

Figure 5-2

To know the facing direction simultaneously provides the sitting direction, and vice versa.

Note: A sitting direction is represented by the symbol   .
        A facing direction is represented by the symbol .

Example 5-8:   Kan House Trigram

Sitting North, Facing South

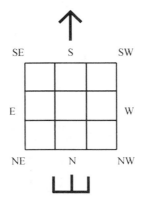

Example 5-9:

Kun House Trigram
Sitting Southwest, Facing Northeast

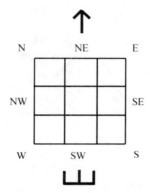

Example 5-10:

Chen House Trigram
Sitting East, Facing West

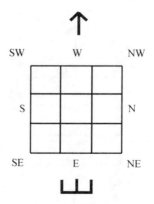

Example 5-11:

Sun House Trigram
Sitting Southeast, Facing Northwest

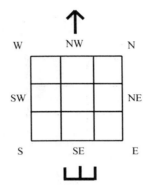

Example 5-12:

Chien House Trigram
Sitting Northwest, Facing Southeast

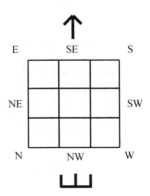

Example 5-13:

Tui House Trigram
Sitting West, Facing East

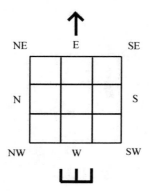

Example 5-14:

Ken House Trigram
Sitting Northeast, Facing Southwest

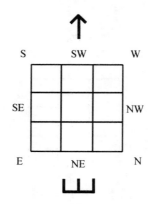

Example 5-15:

Li House Trigram
Sitting South, Facing North

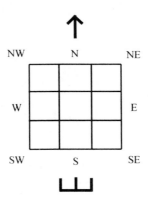

NW   N   NE

W   E

SW   S   SE

Finding Sitting and Facing Directions of Buildings

Measuring and deciding the sitting and facing directions of a house
or building has always been a crucial part of Feng Shui reading that
requires a substantial amount of experience and practice. Keen
observation is also required for such practice. The surroundings of
the house, internal placement, external structure, and its landscape
are all contributing factors when making a judgment on the facing
and sitting sides of a building.   One can follow some general
guidelines to facilitate this task. They are:

1) Main Entrance   Usually on the facing side of building.

2) Traffic	Where traffic is heaviest may be the facing side of building.
3) Interior Placement	Bedrooms or kitchens are normally located on the sitting side of a building; whereas, living rooms and family rooms are often on the facing side.

The above only serve as guidelines and, of course, there are always exceptions to the rule. A good example to illustrate this would be a house with its main entrance on an obscure side, while having a spectacular ocean view on the other. Feng Shui beginners are often confused by this type of unusual house orientation and consequently mistake the side with the main entrance as the facing side of the house. In fact, in this example, the side where the house faces the ocean is the facing side of house. The internal placement of this house that decides the sitting and facing directions. Fortunately, the possibility of coming across houses with "hard to decide" or "unusual" orientations is rare.

From years of teaching, I have discovered that Feng Shui students are most intrigued by how to avoid determining erroneously the sitting and facing sides of a building. To elaborate on the exceptions to the rule is beyond the scope of this book. However, I reiterate that a Feng Shui student must learn from hands-on practice and fieldwork, aside from having a thorough knowledge of the basic theories.

After deciding the facing side of a building, we are now ready to determine the sitting direction of a building using a Lo Pan (羅 盤), a Chinese compass, or a western compass. However, we recommend that readers who want to further their studies in Feng Shui use a Lo Pan.

Practical Skills — Use of a Lo Pan

A Lo Pan is a Chinese compass derived from the teachings of the *Yi-Jing*, *Book of Change*. It is an essential apparatus that no Feng Shui practitioner can do without.

A Lo Pan is a vital device for measuring directions in Feng Shui practice. The Chinese Lo Pan we normally see are pieces of intricate tools in round shapes with a maximum of 36 tiers. Each tier has its own purpose for divination. The original Lo Pan was first invented as a simple tool exclusively for the purpose of finding the four directions, North, South, East and West. Since its invention, the Lo Pan has been modified numerous times, and on its face are now added data related to astronomy, geology, etc.

The Lo Pan, was originally divided into four sections, and later evolved into eight sections. The Eight Trigrams were further developed into 64 hexagrams (sections), with the added information of the Ten Heavenly Stems, Twelve Earthly Branches, Five Elements, celestial bodies, etc. Over the years, the Lo Pan has gradually transformed into a sophisticated tool that is too complicated for the layman.

Our readers need only to concentrate on one of the 36 tiers with the 24 sections on the face of the Lo Pan. The earth is round, as is the design of the Lo Pan. The circumference of its dial is divided into eight directions (sections): North, South, East, West, Northwest, Northeast, Southeast and Southwest. Each direction is assigned with its corresponding trigram: Kan, Li, Chen, Tui, Chien, Ken, Sun, and Kun, respectively. Each trigram (direction) is further evenly distributed into three more sections. Hence there are a total of 24 sections.

The 24 sections are named after the trigrams, the Ten Heavenly Stems, and the Twelve Earthly Branches. The Stems and Branches are discussed in the forthcoming book.

I have redesigned the Lo Pan in view of the complexity of a classic Chinese Lo Pan. Sang's Lo Pan is a simplified, user-friendly version with only 24 sections, designed to enhance and facilitate the reading of a building.

Sang's Lo Pan

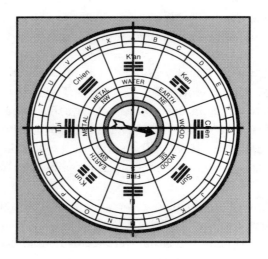

Figure 5-1

The Classic Chinese Lo Pan

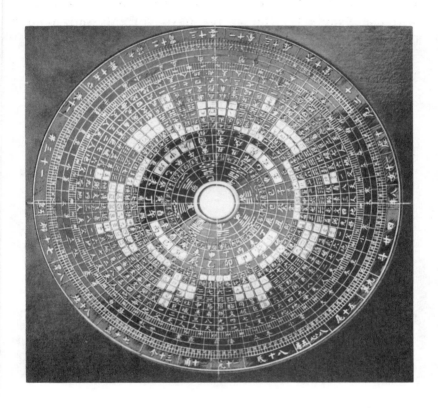

Figure 5-2

A.   Parts of Sang's Lo Pan

Let us review the parts of a Lo Pan. Due to its different versions, we will use Sang's Lo pan as the basis for this introduction (see Figure 5-3).

1)   *Magnetic Arrow*
         The arrowhead points south rather than north as a western compass would.

2)   *North Dots* (twin dots at the center of the rotating dial)
         Always adjust the rotating dial to align the twin dots with the feather-end of the arrow.

3)   *Crosshair Alignments*
         The red crosshairs designate the facing and sitting directions (Trigrams), once the arrow is steady and the feather-end is aligned with the north twin dots.

4)   *Eight Trigrams*
         The Eight Trigrams are the basis for orientation in Feng Shui and are shown on the Lo Pan with their respective elements, symbols, and directions.

5)   *Western Alphabet Designations*
         Each Trigram (direction) is divided into three equal parts. These parts are shown in their Chinese symbols. For easier differentiation, they are shown on Sang's Lo Pan with Western Alphabet Designations.

6)   *Degrees*
         Outermost on the dial are the western compass degrees in arabic numerals.

Parts of Sang's Lo Pan

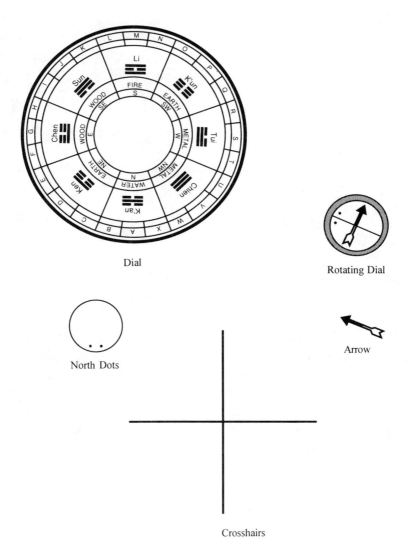

Dial

Rotating Dial

North Dots

Arrow

Crosshairs

Figure 5-3

B.   Proper Procedures on Using Sang's Lo Pan

1)   Determine the facing side of a building. In most cases, the front entrance is located on the facing side. Stand facing the same side that the building faces and align yourself with your back parallel to the facing side and in the center of the building (see Figure 5-4).

2)   Stay a good distance away from any large metal objects such as cars, steel beams or poles, or lamp posts. Remove any heavy jewelry or large metal belt buckles as they will distort your reading.

3)   Stand straight and hold the Lo Pan at waist level. Wait until the arrow stops quivering.

4)   Turn the Lo Pan dial to align the North twin dots with the feather-end of the arrow (see Figure 5-5).

5)   The vertical crosshair indicates the facing and sitting directions of the building. The crosshair end that points toward your body is the sitting direction (trigram). The opposite end indicates the facing direction of the building.

6)   Take at least three separate readings from other positions, all on the facing side; namely, the farthest right, the farthest left and the center of the facing side of the building. Take the result from the CENTER reading if you find discrepancies in different readings.

Figure 5-4

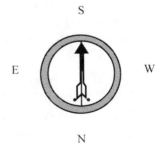

Figure 5-5

C.   Care of a Lo Pan

A Lo Pan should always be treated with the utmost care. Damage of any kind to a Lo Pan will result in faulty measurements and, consequently, distort your reading completely.

1) Always store the Lo Pan face up and in a horizontal position.
2) Keep it away from metal objects or heat.
3) Never leave a Lo Pan in a car.

MATCHING A PERSONAL TRIGRAM WITH A HOUSE TRIGRAM

The basic understanding of Feng Shui is to match one's Personal Trigram with a House Trigram, arriving at an agreeable and complementary state.

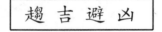

Approach Fortune and Avoid Misfortune

However, should circumstances limit or hinder such accord, the alternative is to match one's bedroom direction with one's Personal Trigram's favorable directions for a bedroom. This will be discussed later.

The tables from Page 71 to 78 explain how one's Personal Trigram is matched with a House Trigram. They will guide you through every one of the Personal Trigrams and examine closely how the eight different House Trigrams affect your health and fortune.

Kan Personal Trigram

House Trigram	Sits	Faces	Interpretations
Sun	SE	NW	A. Good Fortune & Great Fame
Chen	E	W	B. Good Wealth & Helpful Friendships
Li	S	N	C. Family Harmony & Good Public Relationships
Kan	N	S	D. Peace & Good Management
Tui	W	E	E. Arguments & Potential Lawsuits
Chien	NW	SE	F. Misfortunes, Malicious Influences are likely
Ken	NE	SW	G. Accidents, Disasters, Evil Influences
Kun	SW	NE	H. Unproductive Career, Poor Finances, Robberies

Li Personal Trigram

House Trigram	Sits	Faces	Interpretations
Chen	E	W	A. Good Fortune & Great Fame
Sun	SE	NW	B. Good Wealth & Helpful Friendships
Kan	N	S	C. Family Harmony & Good Public Relationships
Li	S	N	D. Peace & Good Management
Ken	NE	SW	E. Arguments & Potential Lawsuits
Kun	SW	NE	F. Misfortunes, Malicious Influences are likely
Tui	W	E	G. Accidents, Disasters, Evil Influences
Chien	NW	SE	H. Unproductive Career, Poor Finances, Robberies

Chen Personal Trigram

House Trigram	Sits	Faces	Interpretations
Li	S	N	A. Good Fortune & Great Fame
Kan	N	S	B. Good Wealth & Helpful Friendships
Sun	SE	NW	C. Family Harmony & Good Public Relationships
Chen	E	W	D. Peace & Good Management
Kun	SW	NE	E. Arguments & Potential Lawsuits
Ken	NE	SW	F. Misfortunes, Malicious Influences are likely
Chien	NW	SE	G. Accidents, Disasters, Evil Influences
Tui	W	E	H. Unproductive Career, Poor Finances, Robberies

Sun Personal Trigram

House Trigram	Sits	Faces	Interpretations
Kan	N	S	A. Good Fortune & Great Fame
Li	S	N	B. Good Wealth & Helpful Friendships
Chen	E	W	C. Family Harmony & Good Public Relationships
Sun	SE	NW	D. Peace & Good Management
Chien	NW	SE	E. Arguments & Potential Lawsuits
Tui	W	E	F. Misfortunes, Malicious Influences are likely
Kun	SW	NE	G. Accidents, Disasters, Evil Influences
Ken	NE	SW	H. Unproductive Career, Poor Finances, Robberies

Chien Personal Trigram

House Trigram	Sits	Faces	Interpretations
Tui	W	E	A. Good Fortune & Great Fame
Ken	NE	SW	B. Good Wealth & Helpful Friendships
Kun	SW	NE	C. Family Harmony & Good Public Relationships
Chien	NW	SE	D. Peace & Good Management
Sun	SE	NW	E. Arguments & Potential Lawsuits
Kan	N	S	F. Misfortunes, Malicious Influences are likely
Chen	E	W	G. Accidents, Disasters, Evil Influences
Li	S	N	H. Unproductive Career, Poor Finances, Robberies

Kun Personal Trigram

House Trigram	Sits	Faces	Interpretations
Ken	NE	SW	A. Good Fortune & Great Fame
Tui	W	E	B. Good Wealth & Helpful Friendships
Chien	NW	SE	C. Family Harmony & Good Public Relationships
Kun	SW	NE	D. Peace & Good Management
Chen	E	W	E. Arguments & Potential Lawsuits
Li	S	N	F. Misfortunes, Malicious Influences are likely
Sun	SE	NW	G. Accidents, Disasters, Evil Influences
Kan	N	S	H. Unproductive Career, Poor Finances, Robberies

Tui Personal Trigram

House Trigram	Sits	Faces	Interpretations
Chien	NW	SE	A. Good Fortune & Great Fame
Kun	SW	NE	B. Good Wealth & Helpful Friendships
Ken	NE	SW	C. Family Harmony & Good Public Relationships
Tui	W	E	D. Peace & Good Management
Kan	N	S	E. Arguments & Potential Lawsuits
Sun	SE	NW	F. Misfortunes, Malicious Influences are likely
Li	S	N	G. Accidents, Disasters, Evil Influences
Chen	E	W	H. Unproductive Career, Poor Finances, Robberies

Ken Personal Trigram

House Trigram	Sits	Faces	Interpretations
Kun	SW	NE	A. Good Fortune & Great Fame
Chien	NW	SE	B. Good Wealth & Helpful Friendships
Tui	W	E	C. Family Harmony & Good Public Relationships
Ken	NE	SW	D. Peace & Good Management
Li	S	N	E. Arguments & Potential Lawsuits
Chen	E	W	F. Misfortunes, Malicious Influences are likely
Kan	N	S	G. Accidents, Disasters, Evil Influences
Sun	SE	NW	H. Unproductive Career, Poor Finances, Robberies

From years of teaching experience, I have developed an Eight Trigram Letter System for non-Chinese-reading students. The eight letters A, B, C, D, E, F, G, and H each represent a certain Qi and magnetic fields for both the Personal Trigrams and House Trigrams.

Letter A

生氣   貪狼
Sheng Qi   astrologically known as   *Tan Lang*
              Wood Element

A is considered most favorable of the eight Qi. Entrances or bedrooms acquire A magnetic field that is good for people, will bring huge fortunes, approach statesmanship, and bring about respectability.

Letter B

天醫   巨門
Tian Yi   astrologically known as   *Ju Men*
              Earth Element

B is the second most favorable. B at entrances or in bedrooms will maintain good health and safety.

Letter   C

延年
Yan Nian   astrologically known as   武曲
Wu Qu

Metal Element

C is most favorable. Entrances or bedrooms with C Qi will acquire a harmonious marital relationship or an early marriage. C is also good for fortune.

Letter D

伏位
Fu Wei   astrologically known as   輔弼
Fu Bi

Wood Element

D is fourth most favorable. You will always find D Qi in the sitting quadrant of a house or, in other words the direction the House Trigram represents. For example, if a house has a north sitting direction, it is a Kan House. The D Qi resides in the northern (sitting) quadrant of this house. As another example, Chien house has a northwest sitting direction. The D Qi is therefore found in the northwest (sitting) quadrant of the house. D in the entrance or bedroom will provide occupants with peace and good management.

Letter E

禍害   祿存
Huo Hai   astrologically known as   *Lu Cun*
Earth Element

E is considered the fourth most unfavorable. If present in entrances or bedrooms, **E** is known to give adverse effects, such as money loss, lawsuits, and arguments.

Letter F

六煞   文曲
Liu Sha   astrologically known as   *Wen Qu*
Water Element

F is third most unfavorable. If it is found present in entrances or bedrooms, it will cause malicious sexual encounters, failed relationships, and arguments.

Letter G

五鬼   廉貞
Wu Gui   astrologically known as   *Lian Zhen*
Fire Element

G is second most unfavorable. If **G** is found present in entrances or bedrooms, it will bring about abandonment by all friends and relatives (親朋背棄), or cause fires and accidents. However, if Wu Gui (Five Ghosts) were manipulated properly using the technique "Five Ghosts Transport Fortune," the home owner could acquire huge and quick fortunes.

Letter H

絕命   破軍
Jue Ming   astrologically known as   *Po Jun*
                    Metal Element

This is the least favorable type of Qi. Avoid using entrances or bedrooms with **H** energy. It is associated with accidents, robberies, and incurable diseases. In all, it is not good for money or people.

A.   Rules and Guidelines to Transforming the Eight Trigrams (Personal and House Trigrams)

We have discussed the different types of Qi and their directions based on Personal and House Trigrams and how they affect our lives in many aspects. Now we will discuss how each trigram is transformed to obtain the eight types of Qi and how to locate them.

Remember each of the Eight Trigrams is made up of three lines. A line could be Yin - - or Yang —. For example, a Chien trigram consists of three Yang lines. The transformation we discuss here involves moving of the lines. Readers who have studied Yi-Jing will find this technique familiar. Moving lines means changing a Yin line to a Yang line, or vice versa. Which line needs to be changed depends solely on which Qi you are trying to locate.

Before we discuss the rules to the transformation, we have to remember that a trigram should be read starting from the line at the bottom. For example, a Chen trigram will have the first line in Yang, the second line in Yin, and the third line in Yin as well.

CHEN TRIGRAM

▬▬ ▬▬	3rd Line
▬▬ ▬▬	2nd Line
▬▬▬▬	1st Line

Example 5-16:

Letter A: *Sheng Qi* - Moving of the 3rd line.

Original Personal/House Trigram is a Chien Trigram:

                    3rd Line

After transforming the 3rd line, a Chien Trigram is changed into a Tui Trigram.

Finding:

The **A** Qi of a Chien Personal/House Trigram is located in the West direction (Tui).

Example 5-17:

Letter B: *Tian Yi* - Changing of both the 1st and 2nd lines.

Original Personal/House Trigram is a Chien Trigram:

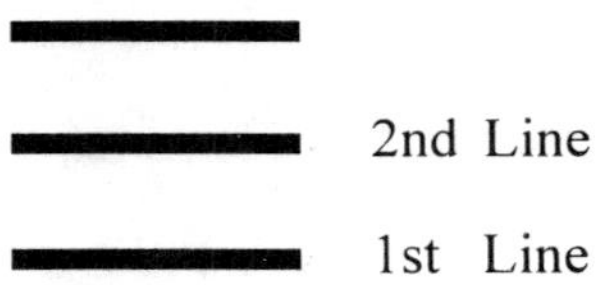

▬▬▬▬▬

▬▬▬▬▬   2nd Line

▬▬▬▬▬   1st   Line

After transforming the 1st and 2nd lines, the Chien Trigram is changed into a Ken Trigram

▬▬▬▬▬

▬▬ ▬▬

▬▬ ▬▬

Finding:

The **B** Qi of a Chien Personal/House Trigram is located in the Northeast direction (Ken).

Example 5-18:

Letter C: *Yan Nian* - Changing of all three lines.

Original Personal/House Trigram is a Chien Trigram.

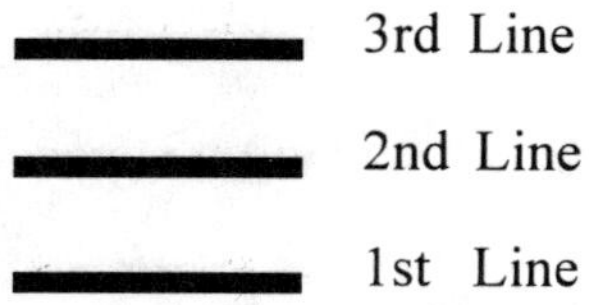

▬▬▬▬▬▬	3rd Line
▬▬▬▬▬▬	2nd Line
▬▬▬▬▬▬	1st Line

After transforming all three lines, the Chien Trigram is now a Kun Trigram.

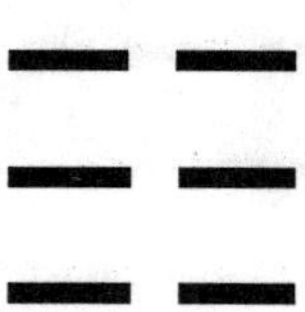

▬▬ ▬▬

▬▬ ▬▬

▬▬ ▬▬

Finding:

The **C** Qi of a Chien Personal/House Trigram is found in the Southwest direction (Kun).

Example 5-19:

Letter D: *Fu Wei* - NO changing of any lines.

Original Personal/House Trigram is a Chien Trigram.

No Change

Since there is no change to any of the lines, the original Chien Trigram remains a Chien Trigram.

Finding:

The **D** Qi of a Chien Personal/House Trigram is found in the Northwest direction (Chien).

Example 5-20:

Letter E: *Huo Hai* - Changing of the 1st line.

Original Personal/House Trigram is a Chien Trigram.

```
━━━━━━━

━━━━━━━

━━━━━━━   1st   Line
```

After transforming the 1st line, the Chien Trigram is now a Sun Trigram.

```
━━━━━━━

━━━━━━━

━━  ━━
```

Finding:

The **E** Qi of a Chien Personal/House Trigram is found in the Southeast direction (Sun).

Example 5-21:

Letter F: *Liu Sha* - Changing of the 1st and 3rd lines.

Original Personal/House Trigram is a Chien Trigram.

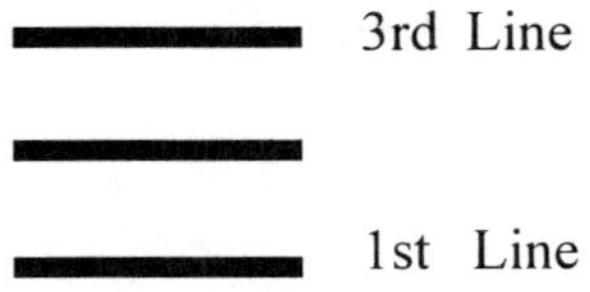

▬▬▬▬▬▬▬   3rd Line

▬▬▬▬▬▬▬

▬▬▬▬▬▬▬   1st Line

After transforming the 1st and 3rd lines, the Chien Trigram is changed into a Kan Trigram.

▬▬ ▬▬

▬▬▬▬▬▬

▬▬ ▬▬

Finding:

The **F** Qi of a Chien Personal/House Trigram is found in the North direction (Kan).

Example 5-22:

Letter G: *Wu Gui* - Changing of the 2nd and 3rd lines.

Original Personal/House Trigram is a Chien Trigram.

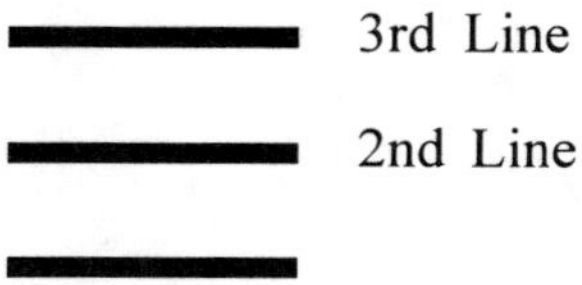

━━━━━━━━   3rd Line

━━━━━━━━   2nd Line

━━━━━━━━

After transforming the 2nd and 3rd lines, the Chien Trigram is changed into a Chen Trigram.

━━ ━━

━━ ━━

━━━━━━━━

Finding:

The **G** Qi of a Chien Personal/House Trigram is found in the East direction (Chen).

Example 5-23:

Letter H: *Jue Ming* - Changing of the 2nd line.

Original Personal/House Trigram is a Chien Trigram.

▬▬▬▬▬

▬▬▬▬▬ 2nd Line

▬▬▬▬▬

After transforming the 2nd line, the Chien Trigram is changed into a Li Trigram.

▬▬▬▬▬

▬▬ ▬▬

▬▬▬▬▬

Finding:

The **H** Qi of a Chien Personal/House Trigram is found in the South direction (Li).

B. Symbologies of the Eight Trigram Letter System

The following is a table summarizing the eight different types of Qi and their symbologies:

A	Good Fortune & Great Fame
B	Good Wealth & Helpful Friendship
C	Family Harmony & Good Public Relationship
D	Peace & Good Management
E	Arguments & Potential Lawsuits
F	Misfortune and Malicious Influences are likely
G	Accidents, Disasters, & Evil Influences
H	Unproductive Careers, Poor Finances, & Robberies

C.   More Examples of Transformation

Original Li Personal/House Trigram.

To find **A:**

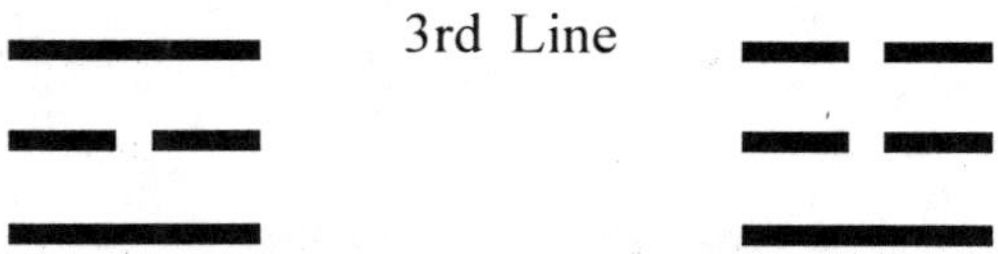

3rd Line

To find **B**:

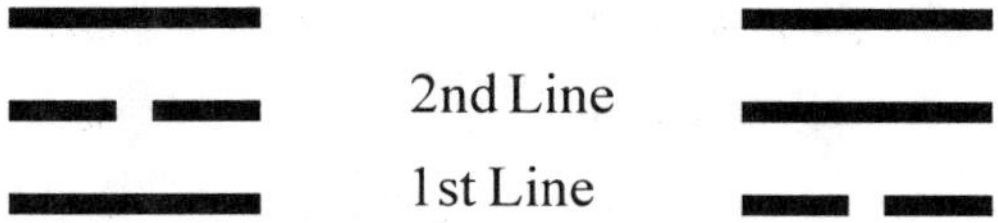

2nd Line
1st Line

To find **C**:

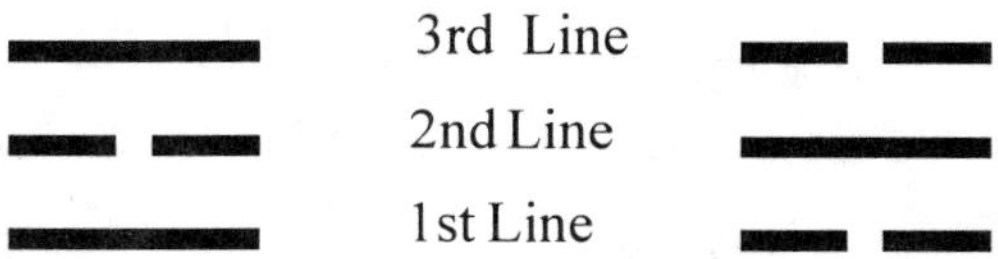

3rd Line
2nd Line
1st Line

To find **D**:

No Change

To find **E**:

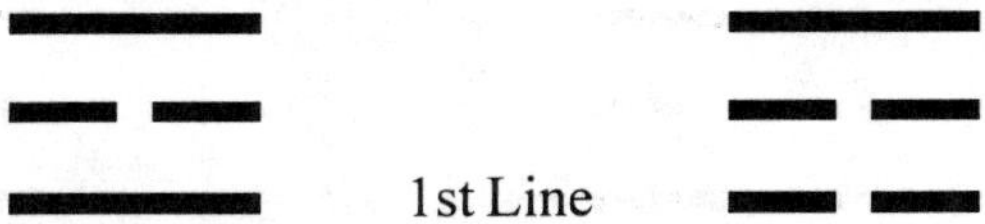

1st Line

To find **F**:

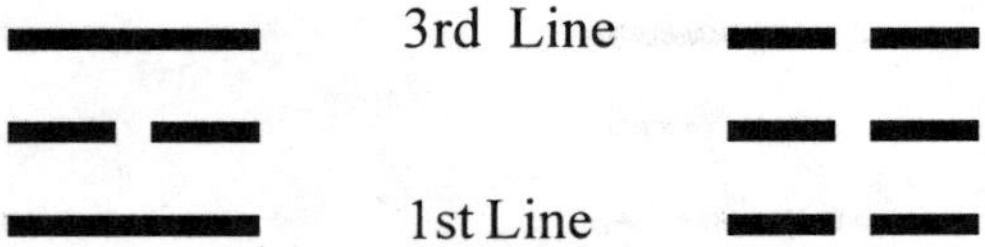

3rd Line

1st Line

To find **G**:

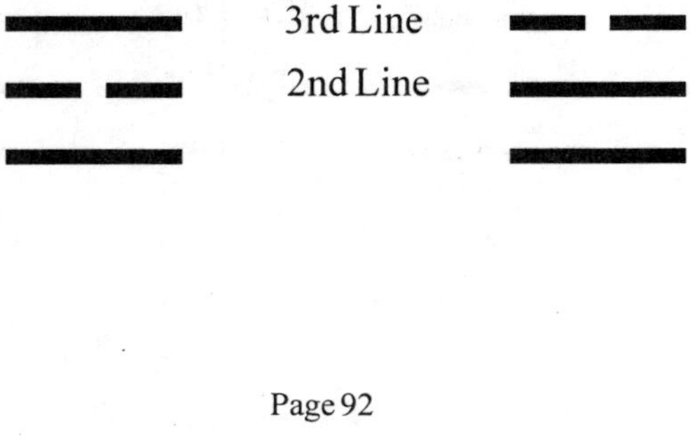

3rd Line

2nd Line

To find **H**:

2nd Line

We have included a quick reference guide for finding the different types of Qi for both the Personal and House Trigrams (see Figures 5-6 to 5-13). Each of the Eight Trigrams is shown under the group (East or West) to which it belongs. The center of each dial is marked with the name of the Trigram.

Example:

A Kun person would look at the dial under the West group with Kun in the center of dial. The dial would tell the Kun individual by the letters A, B, C or D, what is considered favorable. Directions with the letters E, F, G or H are deemed unfavorable.

The same applies to finding the Qi of a house. A house with a south sitting direction is a Li House. The dial would be under the East group and the center should show Li. Again, with the dial, one can find the favorable quadrant for entrances and bedrooms. In this example, the directional quadrant with letters A, B, C, and D are desirable for placing an entrance or a bedroom.

More will be discussed in later chapters.

East Group

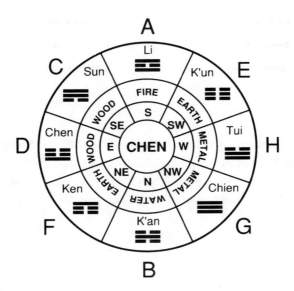

Figure 5-6

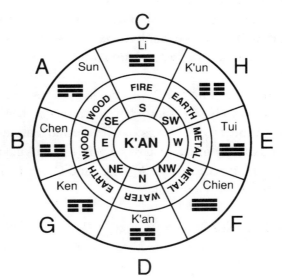

Figure 5-7

East Group

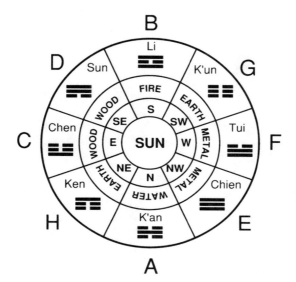

Figure 5-8

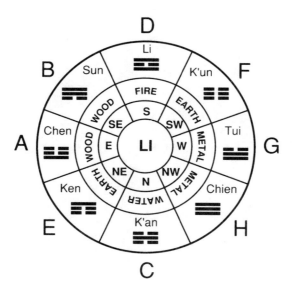

Figure 5-9

West Group

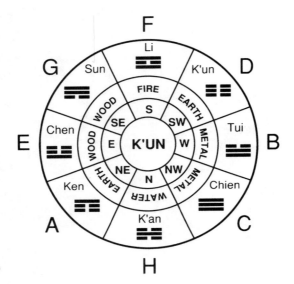

Figure 5-10

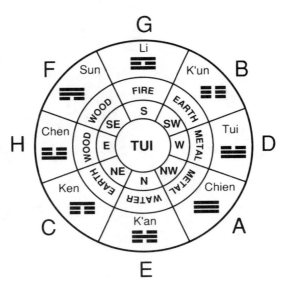

Figure 5-11

West Group

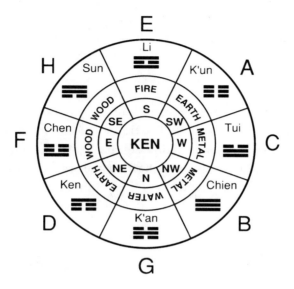

Figure 5-12

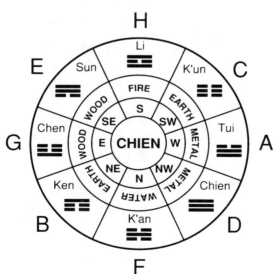

Figure 5-13

Putting the East/West System to Work

After learning how to put the Lo Pan to use and find the sitting direction of a building, we are ready to discuss the necessary preparations before matching a Personal Trigram with a House Trigram.

Step One

First, we should have a floor plan of the building. A sketch is acceptable if it is true to scale. The floor plan should show locations of the building's major and side entrances. The eight directions should be marked accordingly on the floor plan, specifically indicating the sitting and facing directions of the building, to avoid confusion (see Figure 5-14).

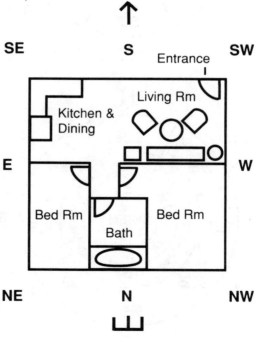

Figure 5-14

Step Two

We now need to draw a blank grid (similar to the Eight Trigram Grid shown in figure 4-2) over the floor plan. The grid should consist of nine quadrants of equal proportion. We suggest that the sketch of the floor plan be large enough to write in the Eight Trigram letters. However, there is one alternative that most of our students choose: the blank grid is prepared as a separate overlay. The grid should be labelled with the eight directions (see Figure 5-15).

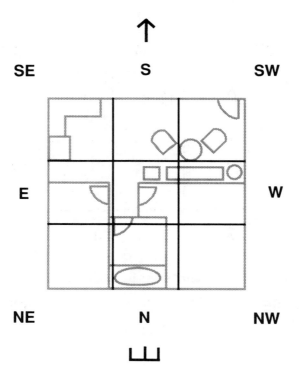

Figure 5-15

Step Three

Knowing the sitting direction of a building will give you the House Trigram; find the dial that belongs to the same House Trigram (see Figures 5-6 to 5-13). Enter the eight letters into its corresponding directional quadrant on the grid. The letters on the overlay are then superimposed onto the floor plan. This way, the floor plan will not look overcrowded with information and the analysis will be easier.

Kan House Trigram

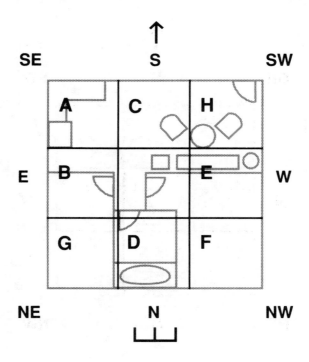

Figure 5-16

Step Four
The next set of letters to enter is the Personal Trigram. Find the occupants' Personal Trigrams by using the formulas shown in Examples 5-2 to 5-7, or refer to the Personal Trigram Quick Reference Guide on page 54 and page 55. We suggest using different colors for different sets of Personal Trigram letters to differentiate what effects the Qi in the building has on each occupant. In this example, we use *Italic* for the Personal Trigram letters.

Kan House Trigram, left side, Normal
Li Personal Trigram, right side, *Italic*

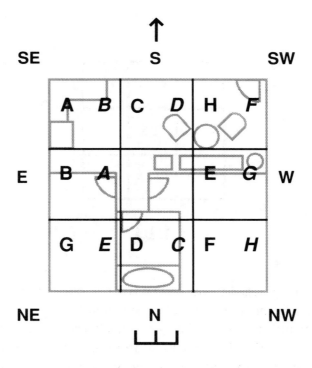

Figure 5-17

We are now ready to move onto the Personal/House Trigram Analysis.

More on the Personal/House Trigram Match

The Sitting and Facing directions always have been the only condition that can decide the effects of a house on its occupants. A House Trigram that is agreeable with a Personal Trigram is the most desirable match and most advantageous to the occupant. A Kun person living in a Kun house (SW sitting and NE facing) is a perfect match, shown as follows:

Kun House Trigram, left side, Normal
Kun Personal Trigram, right side, *Italic*

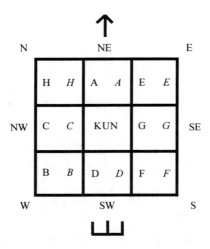

How can one pick and choose when it is not feasible to attain both good sitting and facing directions at the same time? Which will be more important, the sitting or the facing direction? The answer is the sitting direction. A sitting direction decides a House Trigram, and a House Trigram is matched with a Personal Trigram. Its other significance is that a sitting direction can never be altered. Unlike the facing direction, when the entrance is in an unfavorable facing directional quadrant, we can adjust it by using an existing side entrance or by opening another entrance at a more favorable direction (see following example):

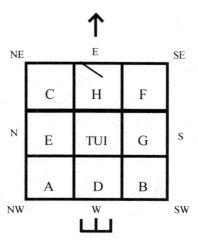

The example above shows a Tui house with an entrance at the facing East quadrant with an **H** (misfortunes and malicious influences are likely).

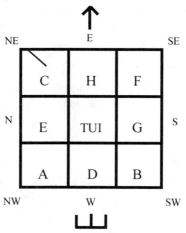

After an adjustment, the example above now shows an entrance at the Northeast quadrant with a **C** (family harmony and good public relationships).

At best, entrances should be positioned in quadrants with A, or in the order of B, C, or D for whichever House Trigram. Avoid having entrances in quadrants with E, F, G, and H. (See page 90 for the symbologies of the Eight Trigram Letter System).

Despite the sitting and facing directions of buildings, some books teach or suggest that all entrances should be positioned on the left side of buildings. Many terms as "Left Green Dragon," "Right White Tiger," etc., are often discussed in these books, but in fact, they convey no importance in Feng Shui. They are only colloquial terms with superficial meanings. Most people believe that such terms foretell the fortunes and misfortunes of a building, as they think that Left Green Dragon symbolizes activity and Right White Tiger suggests immobility. Therefore, having entrances on the left side (Left Green Dragon) of a building is undoubtedly the best direction. For a building with a sitting South and a facing North direction, entrances should be positioned on the left side of the building. If an entrance is placed on the left side, which in this example is the NW quadrant, it has an H directional interpretation. This seriously violates the East/West group match theory. In fact, for a South sitting North facing building, entrances only should be placed in the middle quadrant of the facing side. Entrances positioned on either the left or right quadrants are considered inappropriate. However, there are exceptions to this rule that will be discussed in a later chapter.

Experiences have proven that in East sitting West facing Chen Trigram houses, with entrances positioned in the left quadrant (the Kun quadrant with an E), there are frequent quarrels and disagreements between husbands and wives or within the family. An improvement would be to use a side entrance at the Li (south) quadrant.

SPOUSAL PERSONAL TRIGRAM AND HOUSE TRIGRAM MATCH

In previous chapters, we have discussed why an East group person should live in an East group house, and why a West group person should live in a West group house. The East/West group match is believed to have the same effect on relationships. As a rule, it is best for an East group person to marry another East group person. A West group person should be with a West group person. Relationships between people of different groups are often poor and non-communicative. Experiences show that the first born of a West group Chien (Metal Element) Trigram male and an East group Chen (Wood Element) Trigram female, is usually of poor health and may even meet with premature death, due to the domination of metal over wood.

How do we improve Feng Shui for people who have married people of the opposite group, such as East to West, and vice versa? The most straightforward solution is to have separate bedrooms. While this may not be feasible or the easiest solution may not always be the best one, there is another alternative. One would need to determine if the direction of the master bedroom is more in favor of the husband or the wife by matching their Personal Trigrams' favorable bedroom directions to the actual bedroom's direction. When you know the result, position the direction of the bed to compromise with the better direction of the disadvantaged party (see the following pages).

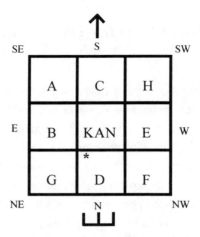

A Kan Trigram house with a North sitting and South facing direction belongs to the East group. The master bedroom is located at the North quadrant of the house with a D (marked with an *). This is considered a favorable quadrant for a bedroom.

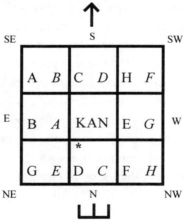

In this same Kan House, we have now input the wife's personal data who belongs to the Li Trigram of the East group. C (family harmony and good public relationship) is found in the North quadrant where the master bedroom is located. This shows that the quadrant is a favorable bedroom direction for the wife.

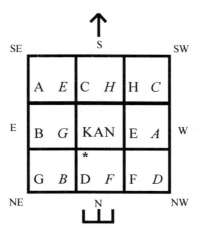

The same Kan House now shows the husband's personal data who belongs to the Chien Trigram of the West group. F (misfortune and malicious influence) is found in the bedroom quadrant; therefore, this bedroom is unfavorable for the husband.

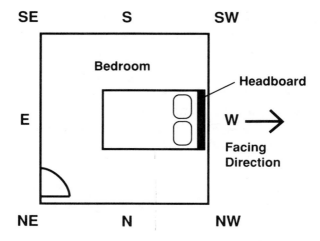

Figure 5-18

Figure 5-18 shows an enlarged quadrant of the bedroom. The bed positioned in the "crown/pillow direction" facing west is the remedy for the husband who, in this example, is the disadvantaged one and west is one of the approved directions for those belonging to the West group.

Entrances

The most important part of a house a Feng Shui practitioner needs to analyze when reading a building is the entrance. The entrance carries great significance in Feng Shui since the entrance is the opening. Qi would flow in and then remain in the house, regardless of the good or bad nature of the Qi, the main concern on which we base our judgment. Knowing how to manipulate Qi by letting it come in through a good entrance direction has always been an efficient method to enhance the fortune and health of a home's occupants.

To achieve a good entrance, one must position in a quadrant that has an approved direction. Entrances are always best if positioned in quadrants with Letter A. Compared to the size of a house or building, an entrance cannot be proportionately too tall (see figure 5-19), too big (see figure 5-20), or too low (see figure 5-21). No entrance should be positioned directly under a ceiling beam (see figure 5-22). Avoid any telephone or power poles erected in front of the entrance. Trim down trees that overshadow or that shut out sunlight to the entrance of a house.

For the East group houses, entrances should be placed in the south quadrant of a Chen Trigram house; north quadrant of a Sun Trigram house; east quadrant of a Li Trigram house; and southeast quadrant of a Kan Trigram house.

West group houses need to position entrances at the northeast quadrant of a Kun Trigram house; northwest quadrant of a Tui Trigram house; west quadrant of the Chien Trigram house; and the southwest quadrant of the Ken Trigram house.

As previously mentioned, entrances should be located in quadrants with A, B, C or D.

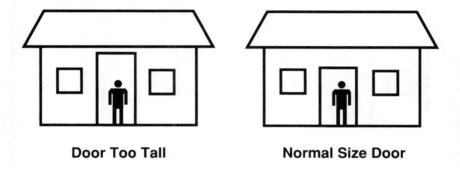

Door Too Tall   **Normal Size Door**

Figure 5-19

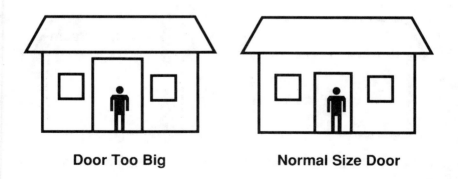

Door Too Big   **Normal Size Door**

Figure 5-20

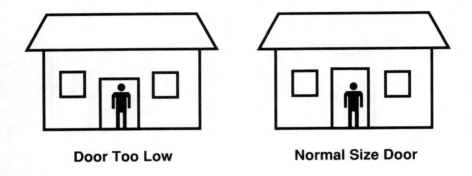

Door Too Low   **Normal Size Door**

Figure 5-21

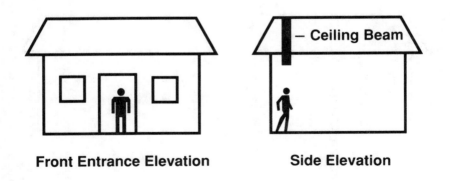

Front Entrance Elevation   **Side Elevation**

Figure 5-22

Bedrooms

After a hard day, the bedroom is a significant place to rest and regain energy. In Feng Shui, a bedroom is extremely important. A sound, good night's sleep helps to revitalize one's body with energy and a clear mind. Therefore, a bedroom besides influencing one's health and posterity also affects one's career and luck.

The first requirement for choosing a bedroom is to match the Personal Trigram with the House Trigram. Select a direction from the Personal Trigram that is desirable for a bedroom. Bedrooms are best to be positioned in areas with Letter D. The best directions for East and West group people are as follows:

For an East group person

Favorable directions :   East, Southeast, South, and North
Unfavorable directions : West, Southwest, Northwest, and Northeast

For a West group person

Favorable directions: West, Southwest, Northwest, and Northeast
Unfavorable directions: East, Southeast, South, and North

Bedrooms are best in quadrants with D, C, B and A.

The following are guidelines for East and West group people choosing favorable bedroom directions.

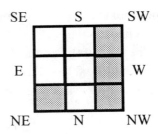

Each square represents a bedroom unit and a direction. The unmarked squares represent the "East Four Rooms," which are the favorable directions for all East group individuals; whereas the shaded squares, represent unfavorable directions for their bedroom placements.

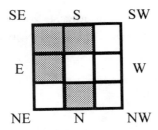

Here, each square again represents a bedroom unit and a direction. The unmarked squares represent the "West Four Rooms" for West group individuals choosing a bedroom with favorable directions. The shaded squares represent unfavorable directions for their bedroom placements.

If an East group person resides in a "West Four House Trigram" house, or a West group individual in a "East Four House Trigram" house, we regard this as a major and most fundamental mistake in Feng Shui. In such situations, the homeowners can match their Personal Trigrams' favorable bedroom directions with the House Trigrams' bedroom directions. In worse circumstances, when even the House Trigram's bedroom directions do not match with the Personal Trigram's, the last resort is to use the "direction of the bed" or the "direction of crown/ pillow" to compromise with the Personal Trigram's favorable directions for bedrooms. Aside from matching the bedroom direction with the Personal Trigram direction, all doors to the bedrooms should be positioned according to the Personal Trigram's favorable bedroom directions. Should the Personal Trigram match with the House Trigram, bedroom directions, and door directions, this fulfills the basic requirements of a desirable bedroom.

Other Concerns of a Bedroom

A bedroom is especially significant to one's well being. It is best in a rectangular or square shape; avoid triangular, irregular, or round shapes. Also avoid steep ceilings. The room must be well ventilated and well lit. It should be neither too dark nor too bright. The room cannot be stifling and should be odor-free. One should avoid putting too many mirrors in a bedroom, particularly not at the end side of a bed as it faces the bed. Mirrors do not belong to any of the Five Elements in Feng Shui and are not considered a remedy for bad Qi (see figure 5-23).

Figure 5-23

Mirrors should not be positioned facing the bed, particularly not at the end side.

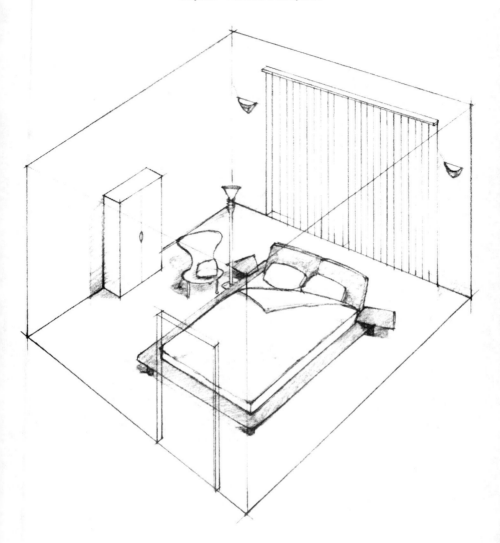

Figure 5-24

The doorway of the bedroom should not face the bed.

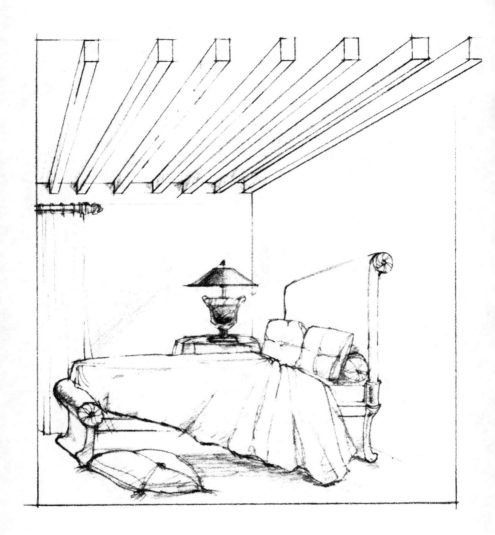

Figure 5-25

Avoid positioning the bed beneath any beams.

SE   S   SW

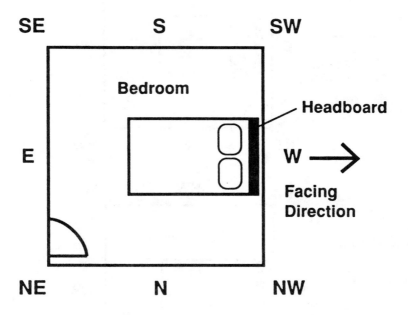

NE   N   NW

Figure 5-26

Generally, one-third of our lifetime is spent in sleep or in repose. In order to sleep comfortably and rest well, one's bed should be positioned to match with the favorable bedroom direction of the Personal Trigram. The position of a bed is decided by either the direction of bed or the direction of crown/pillow.

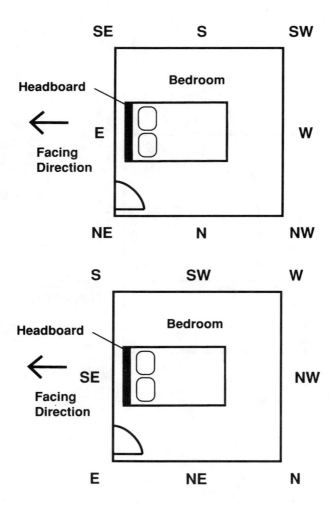

Figure 5-27

East group people should position their beds facing east, southeast, south, or north.

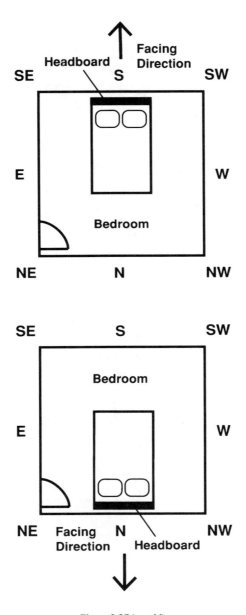

Figure 5-27 (cont'd)

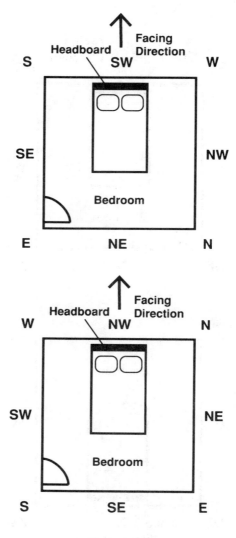

Figure 5-28

West group individuals should position their beds facing west, southwest northwest, or northeast.

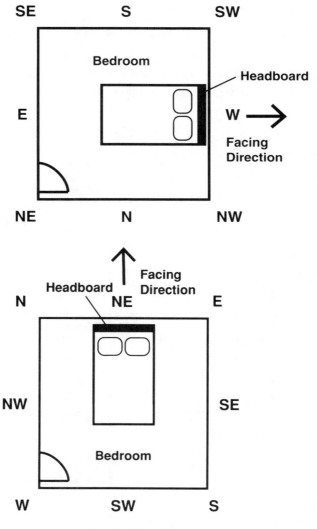

Figure 5-28 (cont'd)

The foremost color theme for bedrooms also needs to coincide with the elemental color(s) associated with one's Personal Trigram (see following charts). Use colors of a productive nature to the element of your Personal Trigram or of the same element group. No colors should dominate your Personal Trigram. Also, avoid colors that will cause any reductive action (see figures 5-29, 5-30 and 5-31).

Personal Trigram/ (Element)	Preferable Colors (Element)	Reason	Not Preferable Colors (Element)	Reason
Chen & Sun (Wood)	1) Lt Blue (Water)	Water Produces Wood	1) Gold (Metal)	Metal Dominates Wood
	2) Lt Green (Wood)	Same Element Wood	2) Red (Fire)	Fire Reduces Wood
Kun & Ken (Earth)	1) Red (Fire)	Fire Produces Earth	1) Lt Green (Wood)	Wood Dominates Earth
	2) Yellow (Earth)	Same Element Earth	2) Gold (Metal)	Metal Reduces Earth
Chien & Tui (Metal)	1) Yellow (Earth)	Earth Produces Metal	1) Red (Fire)	Fire Dominates Metal
	2) Gold (Metal)	Same Element Metal	2) Lt Blue (Water)	Water Reduces Metal
Kan (Water)	1) Gold (Metal)	Metal Produces Water	1) Yellow (Earth)	Earth Dominates Water
	2) Lt Blue (Water)	Same Element Water	2) Lt Green (Wood)	Wood Reduces Water
Li (Fire)	1) Lt Green (Wood)	Wood Produces Fire	1) Lt Blue (Water)	Water Dominates Fire
	2) Red (Fire)	Same Element Fire	2) Yellow (Earth)	Earth Reduces Fire

COLORS OF THE FIVE ELEMENTS

The Productive Cycle

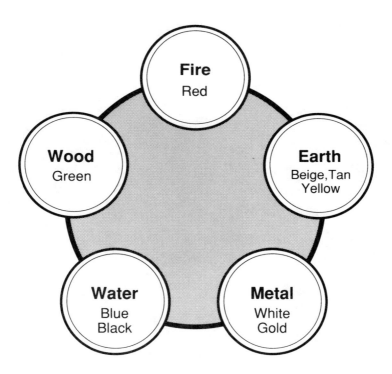

Figure 5-29

COLORS OF THE FIVE ELEMENTS

The Domination Cycle

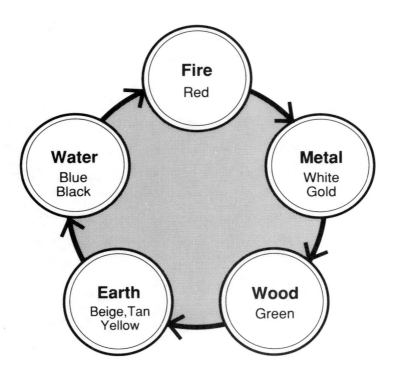

Figure 5-30

COLORS OF THE FIVE ELEMENT

The Reductive Cycle

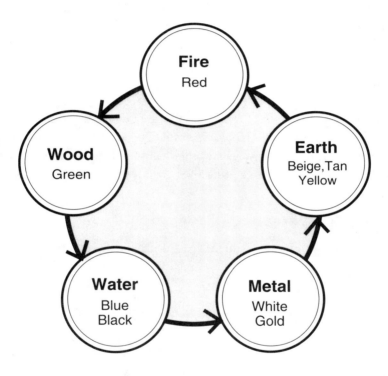

Figure 5-31

KITCHEN AND STOVE

The kitchen and stove have always been an essential part of a house but is often overlooked in today's Feng Shui analysis. It is not a part of the house where you entertain, nor is it an area where you are likely to spend more than a few hours daily. The kitchen is where you prepare one of life's necessities: FOOD. Food, as we know, is a multifaceted necessity in our lives. For the less fortunate, food is for survival. Food for the more fortunate means growth, energy and health. Most of the time, food is simply pleasure.

The kitchen or stove is best placed in an area where the least desirable Qi is, according to one's House Trigram. This way, the fire made when preparing meals will burn off the undesirable and negative Qi collected in the house. They are areas with E, F, G and H from the Eight Trigram Letter System.

If the House Trigram is Kun, the least desirable directions are:

E - East
F - South
G - Southeast
H - North

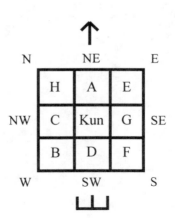

Since East, South, Southeast, and North are the least favorable directions for a Kun person, these would also be appropriate locations for the kitchen and stove.

We have discussed choosing the sitting directions for a kitchen and stove. They are to be put in the least favorable locations according to the House Trigram. But the facing direction of the stove "Fire Door" (火門), should be one of the four favorable directions, according to the HouseTrigram.

In earlier times, before electricity or gas, burning wood or coal was the major energy source for stoves. Earthen stoves were often left with a big frontal opening where wood or coal could be put. The side where the opening faces is the "Fire Door" and is the facing direction of the stove (see figure 5-32).

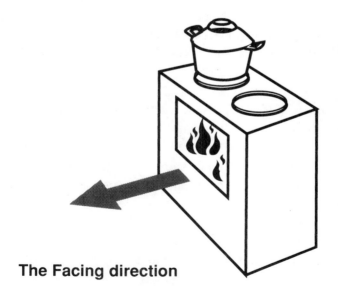

The Facing direction

Figure 5-32

Should the stove face an unfavorable direction, the house's occupants may experience health problems. Feng Shui practitioners often suggest that the kitchen be repositioned, and the stove should face a direction that would help to improve health, since Chinese medicine is based largely on boiling herbs . From past experiences, stoves with a B (Tian-Yi) facing direction enhances the effectiveness of the medicine.

Highly skilled, experienced Feng Shui masters can reverse a home-owner's grave financial situations by making changes to the kitchen. On a carefully selected date and time, the stove would be removed from its original direction and repositioned in a part of the house where the G (Five Ghosts) resides (note that the G is from the House Trigram and not the Personal Trigram). The stove should also be positioned to face the A direction. In order for this move to be effective, it MUST occur when the annual number 8 (see Chapter 6 on Xuan Kong System) enters the G part of the house. Normally, the financial shift takes place in a few days and no later than half a month.

Under the suggestions of Feng Shui practitioners, we have heard of people who spend enormous sums of money restructuring their kitchens. However, one must be extremely cautious about unqualified Feng Shui "masters" who are not knowledgeable about relocating the kitchen to the G part of a house, not to mention picking the right time and date to commence such construction.

One American Feng Shui Institute's student before attending our class, once hired a Feng Shui practitioner who told him that he needed to remodel his existing kitchen and reposition the stove.

After spending approximately $30,000 to have the kitchen remodelled and the stove repositioned according to the practitioner's instructions, he ran into worse financial situations and eventually sold his house. After this student graduated from our Feng Shui Beginning Class, he realized that his kitchen had been placed in an inappropriate part of the house.

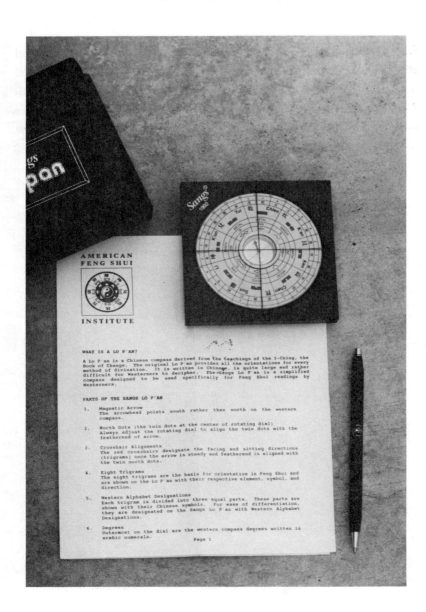

AMERICAN
FENG SHUI

INSTITUTE

WHAT IS A LO P'AN?

A Lo P'an is a Chinese compass derived from the teachings of the I-Ching, the Book of Change. The original Lo P'an provides all the orientations for every method of divination. It is written in Chinese, is quite large and rather difficult for Westerners to decipher. The Sangs Lo P'an is a simplified compass designed to be used specifically for Feng Shui readings by Westerners.

PARTS OF THE SANGS LO P'AN

1. Magnetic Arrow
   The arrowhead points south rather than north on the western compass.

2. North Dots (the twin dots at the center of rotating dial)
   Always adjust the rotating dial to align the twin dots with the featherend of arrow.

3. Crosshair Alignments
   The red crosshairs designate the facing and sitting directions (trigrams) once the arrow is steady and featherend is aligned with the twin north dots.

4. Eight Trigrams
   The eight trigrams are the basis for orientation in Feng Shui and are shown on the Lo P'an with their respective element, symbol, and direction.

5. Western Alphabet Designations
   Each trigram is divided into three equal parts. These parts are shown with their Chinese symbols. For ease of differentiation, they are designated on the Sangs Lo P'an with Western Alphabet Designations.

6. Degrees
   Outermost on the dial are the western compass degrees written in arabic numerals.

Page 1

Page 130

THE SHYUAN K'UNG SYSTEM

THE XUAN KONG SYSTEM

What is Xuan Kong?

You may have questions on what has been previously discussed. Why have we mentioned the Five Elements and their three cycles; what are their uses as far as the East/West System is concerned? Why is the grid used for Feng Shui analysis divided into nine quadrants, leaving the quadrant in the center unattended? What if the bedroom happens to be in this center quadrant?

Most of the answers - to these questions will be found in this chapter. What is Xuan Kong? How does it relate to Feng Shui practice and the Ba Zhai — Eight Trigram House? And in what aspect?

You could call Xuan Kong another system of Feng Shui. It uses numbers derived from the mathematics of Yi-Jing. Xuan Kong is incorporated with the East/West System to achieve a more detailed, comprehensive analysis. Most practitioners who know and are practicing the East/West System may not necessarily know the Xuan Kong system. Those who exercise Xuan Kong undoubtedly also know the East/West system. Students at our Institute often ask which of the two systems is more important when practicing Feng Shui. The answer is that they both share the same significance, because Xuan Kong fills the missing piece of the East/West system — the center quadrant.

More About Xuan Kong

A.   The Solar System and Its Influences on Us

Two thousand years ago, Chinese Feng Shui teaching — through observations — knew of the essence of planetary movements: the Sun, the moon, and their influence and dominance over the earth and its inhabitants. Using this knowledge, accompanied with astrological and geological insight, the trigrams and their corresponding properties were created. Mathematical formulas were then incorporated to select proper places and auspicious times.

The revolving of the moon and sun, the interplay of Yin and Yang, and the interactions between space and the directions all contribute to the vast atmospheric changes of the earth. The magnetic field of the earth varies according to changes in weather. Magnetic field changes directly and indirectly impose influences on all living things on earth.

Beehives are hexagonal, and so are snowflakes. Nearly all mineral crystals have six cubic planes or are in multiples of six. One complete rotation of the earth around the sun is twelve revolutions of the moon around the earth. The lunar calendar comprises twelve months. Many ancient architecture were constructed with twelve floors. Twelve Troy ounces in one pound, twelve inches in a foot, and twelve in a dozen are all multiples of six. Chinese have long used twelve animals to represent the cycle of twelve years in their horoscope. These all prominently show that there is a universal law and order in nature.

B.   Xuan Kong System AKA Zi-Bai Fu

Unlike the eight-lettered East/West system, Xuan Kong is a nine-number system. Like the letters in the East/West system, the numbers are Qi with respective interpretations. The system we will review in this chapter is a dual number system. Each of the nine quadrants, after the floating, will result in a set of two numbers: the House Trigram Number and the Annual Number.

The Eight Trigram Grid

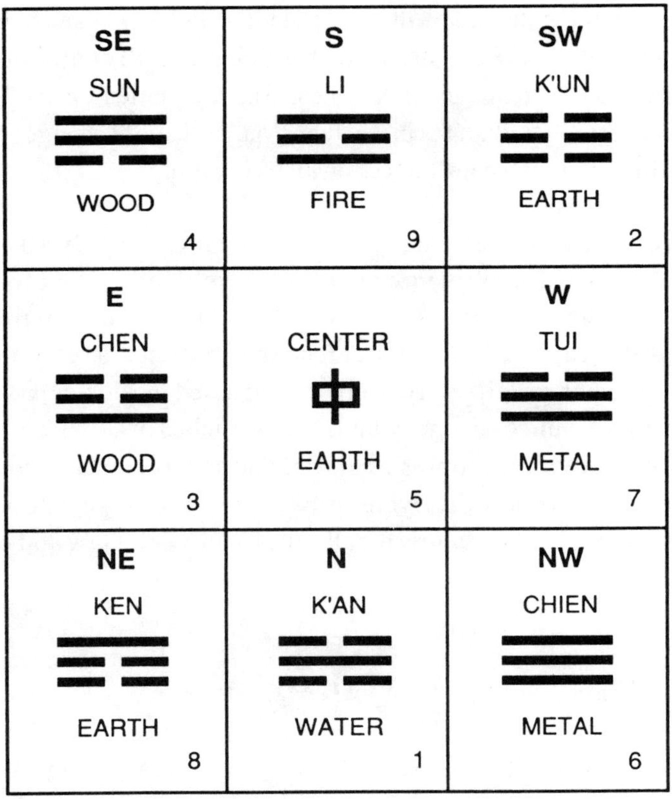

SE	S	SW
SUN	LI	K'UN
☴	☲	☷
WOOD	FIRE	EARTH
4	9	2
E	**CENTER**	**W**
CHEN	中	TUI
☳		☱
WOOD	EARTH	METAL
3	5	7
NE	**N**	**NW**
KEN	K'AN	CHIEN
☶	☵	☰
EARTH	WATER	METAL
8	1	6

Figure 6-1

Figure 6-1 illustrates the Eight Trigram grid. The nine quadrants of the grid are listed with their respective properties, direction, element, and number. Also, each quadrant is assigned one of the Eight Trigrams, except the center quadrant, which has no representing trigram. It represents the central direction and is assigned with an earth element and the number five.

Besides being a number system, Zi-Bai Fu also assigns colors to each of the nine numbers. Since the colors assigned were solely to facilitate learning in ancient times, we will not discuss the Zi-Bai colors here to avoid confusing readers those colors with the Elemental Colors of the Eight Trigrams (see Chapter Four on The Eight Trigrams).

Zi-Bai Fu is known as "Nine Palace Floating Stars" (九宮飛星). As the name implies, it involves the floating of numbers (stars) in the nine quadrants (palaces). There is a mandatory sequence to floating the nine numbers. Let us take another look at Figure 6-1. This time we will concentrate only on the numbers and disregard the other properties of the quadrants. The Nine Palace Floating Stars system always starts at the center. Later in this chapter, we will discuss the proper sequence to float the numbers into the nine quadrants.

The Quadrant	Trigram	Corresponding Number
Central		represented by 5
Northwest	Chien	represented by 6
West	Tui	represented by 7
Northeast	Ken	represented by 8
South	Li	represented by 9
North	Kan	represented by 1
Southwest	Kun	represented by 2
East	Chen	represented by 3
Southeast	Sun	represented by 4

SE	S	SW

4	9	2
3	5	7
8	1	6

E — left of middle row, W — right of middle row

NE	N	NW

The numbers in the Eight Trigram Grid should total as follows:

diagonally from upper left to lower right	(4 + 5 + 6) = 15
diagonally from upper right to lower left	(2 + 5 + 8) = 15
horizontally from upper left to right	(4 + 9 + 2) = 15
horizontally from middle left to right	(3 + 5 + 7) = 15
horizontally from lower left to right	(8 + 1 + 6) = 15
vertically from top right to bottom right	(2 + 6 + 7) = 15
vertically from middle top to bottom left	(9 + 5 + 1) = 15
vertically from top left to bottom left	(4 + 3 + 8) = 15

The Floating

As complicated as it looks, the floating is quite simple. We suggest that readers who seriously want to practice Feng Shui learn the floating sequence by heart.

Here, we discuss the floating in ascending order. We start the floating by putting the first number, which can be any of the nine numbers, into the Central (or center) quadrant, followed by the next number in the Northwest quadrant. The third and the following numbers should go into the West, Northeast, South, North, Southwest, East, and Southeast quadrants respectively.

Summary:

First number into Central quadrant.
Second number into Northwest quadrant.
Third number into West quadrant.
Fourth number into Northeast quadrant.
Fifth number into South quadrant.
Sixth number into North quadrant.
Seventh number into Southwest quadrant.
Eighth number into East quadrant.
Ninth number into Southeast quadrant.

Remember:

1)   First, Second, Third, Fourth...Ninth numbers, are not to be read as the actual numbers 1, 2, 3, 4 . . . . , 9.

2)   To ensure the floating is correct, check the 9th number in the Southeast corner quadrant, also the last quadrant in the floating sequence. It should always have the preceding number to the

number in the Central quadrant. For example, if 8 is the 9th number and floated into the Southeast (last) quadrant, one MUST find 9 in the Central quadrant. Should 9 go into the Southeast quadrant, number 1 should be in the Central quadrant.

What decides which number should go first into the Central quadrant? The answer is the House Trigram type. Remember lessons learned about the East/West system: The type of house is decided by its House Trigram or, in other words, the sitting direction of the house. A north sitting direction house is a Kan house. Kan is represented by the number 1 (see Chapter Five on The East/West system).

Important: A common mistake among most beginners is when they float, they tend to memorize the sequence by their positions in the Eight Trigram grid, e.g. lowest left-hand corner, middle right-hand quadrant and lowest left-hand corner, etc., rather than by the directions. This will throw off the whole floating system. Grids in the samples given in this book are usually oriented with the south direction pointing upward, north downward, east on the left, and west on the right, etc. The grids do not represent any particular House Trigram type unless otherwise specified with both the sitting and facing symbols. Always remember the floating of numbers is a direction-based system.

Example 6-1:

House Trigram Type — Kan House (represented by Number 1)

First Step

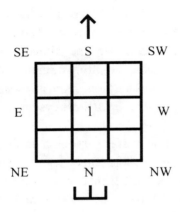

Second Step

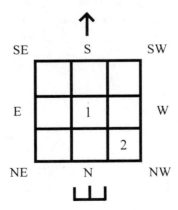

Third Step

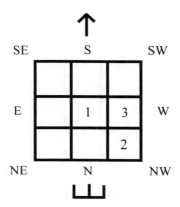

Fourth Step

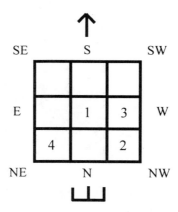

Fifth Step

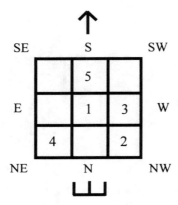

Sixth Step

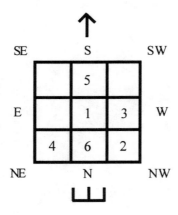

Seventh Step

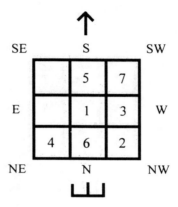

Eight Step

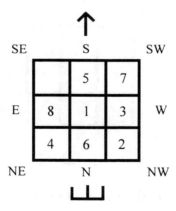

Ninth Step

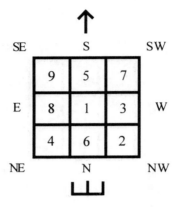

Final Step

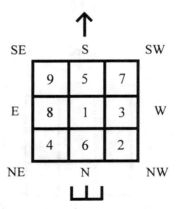

Check the Southeast quadrant to see if its number precedes the number in the Central quadrant. In this example, 9 in the Southeast quadrant precedes 1 in the Central quadrant.

Example 6-2:

House Trigram Type — Tui House (represented by number 7)

First Step

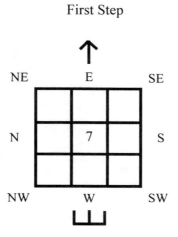

Second Step

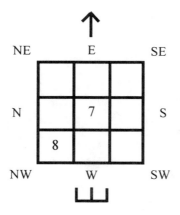

Third Step

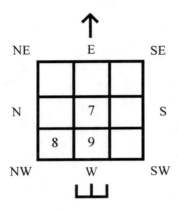

Fourth Step

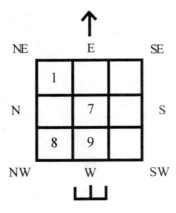

Fifth Step

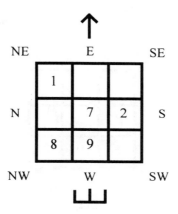

Sixth Step

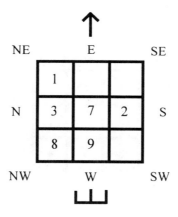

Seventh Step

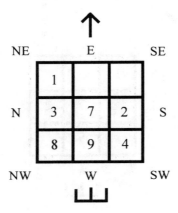

Eighth Step

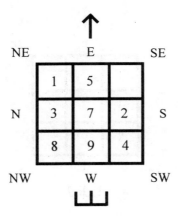

Ninth Step

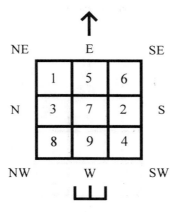

Final Step

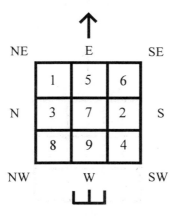

Check to see if the number in the Southeast quadrant precedes the number in the Central quadrant. In this example, 6 in the Southeast quadrant precedes 7 in the Central quadrant.

The following pages are a Quick Reference Guide for the number floating of the Eight Trigram Houses.

Kan House

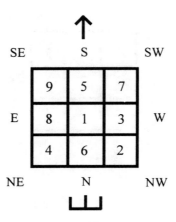

Kun House

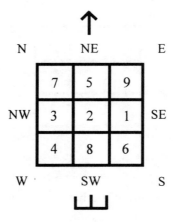

Chen House

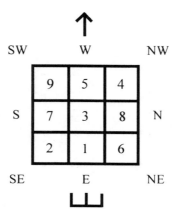

Sun House

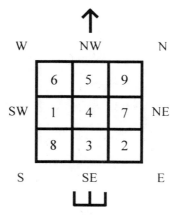

Chien House

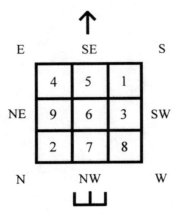

Tui House

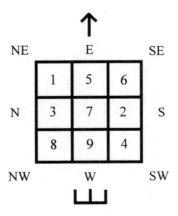

Ken House

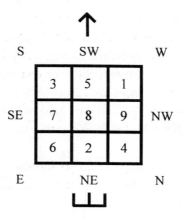

Li House

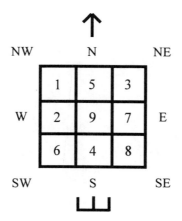

The Second Number — The Annual Number

As mentioned, the Xuan Kong System presented in this book is a dual number system. In addition to the House Trigram number, the other number to be floated into the grid is an annual number signifying the magnetic field changes given out annually by the solar system. You will need to look up the annual number from the quick reference chart (see page 157), which is equivalent to the year you are in when analyzing a specific house. Please always note that February 5th is the cut off day of Chinese calendar year. Should you analyze a house on January 15th, 1993, use the number 8 that falls under the year 1992 on the chart.

The mandatory floating sequence also applies to the annual number. Again, in ascending order, the annual number should be floated in the grid as on the following pages.

Example 6-3:

Year 1992 — Annual number is 8

SE   S   SW

7	3	5
6	8	1
2	4	9

E (left of top row)   W (right of middle row)

NE   N   NW

8 into Central quadrant.
9 into Northwest quadrant.
1 into West quadrant.
2 into Northeast quadrant.
3 into South quadrant.
4 into North quadrant.
5 into Southwest quadrant.
6 into East quadrant.
7 into Southeast quadrant.

Example 6-4:

Year 1994 — Annual number is 6

```
      SE        S        SW

      ┌────┬────┬────┐
      │ 5  │ 1  │ 3  │
      ├────┼────┼────┤
   E  │ 4  │ 6  │ 8  │  W
      ├────┼────┼────┤
      │ 9  │ 2  │ 7  │
      └────┴────┴────┘

      NE        N        NW
```

6 into Central quadrant.
7 into Northwest quadrant.
8 into West quadrant.
9 into Northeast quadrant.
1 into South quadrant.
2 into North quadrant.
3 into Southwest quadrant.
4 into East quadrant.
5 into Southeast quadrant.

The Annual Number Chart

Year	Annual No.	Year	Annual No.
1940	6	1980	2
1941	5	1981	1
1942	4	1982	9
1943	3	1983	8
1944	2	1984	7
1945	1	1985	6
1946	9	1986	5
1947	8	1987	4
1948	7	1988	3
1949	6	1989	2
1950	5	1990	1
1951	4	1991	9
1952	3	1992	8
1953	2	1993	7
1954	1	1994	6
1955	9	1995	5
1956	8	1996	4
1957	7	1997	3
1958	6	1998	2
1959	5	1999	1
1960	4	2000	9
1961	3	2001	8
1962	2	2002	7
1963	1	2003	6
1964	9	2004	5
1965	8	2005	4
1966	7	2006	3
1967	6	2007	2
1968	5	2008	1
1969	4	2009	9
1970	3	2010	8
1971	2	2011	7
1972	1	2012	6
1973	9	2013	5
1974	8	2014	4
1975	7	2015	3
1976	6	2016	2
1977	5	2017	1
1978	4	2018	9
1979	3	2019	8

COMBINING THE TWO NUMBERS

This dual number system consists of a House Trigram Number and an Annual Number. Since there will be two numbers in each quadrant, to avoid confusion while analyzing, we suggest first setting up your own system by deciding which number to float first and what number will sit on the right or left side of the quadrant. Use different colors to distinguish the two sets of numbers. Once you develop a system, stay with it.

Example 6-5:
Analyzing a Kan House in the year 1993
House Trigram Number = 1 (center quadrant, left side), Normal
Annual number   = 7 (in center quadrant, right side), *Italic*

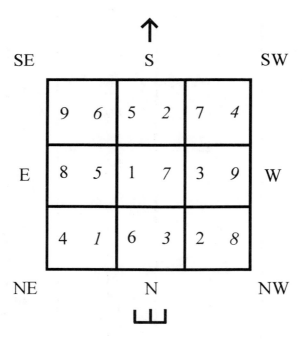

How to Analyze

To determine the fortune and misfortune of each quadrant of a house, the elemental interaction between the two numbers and the symbologies of the numbers should be considered during analysis.

The original symbology of numbers are listed as follows:

<u>Numbers</u>
1: Wealth & powerful position
2: Pain, sickness, miscarriage, & loneliness
3: Gossip, arguments, and lawsuits
4: Scholastic achievement, writing, reading, creativity, promotions & career advancement
5: Fire, sickness, pain, casualties, obstacles, delays, and accidents
6: Great wealth, and authority (although possibly without power)
7: Robbery, imprisonment, fire, bleeding, slander, and arguments
8: Fame wealth & name
9: Enhances accompanying number

1, 4, 6, 8 are favorable.
2, 3, 5, 7 are unfavorable.
9 enhances the number it is with, whether favorably or unfavorably.

Special Number Combinations

Favorable Number Combinations:

1,4 -   Good for studying, examinations, writing, fame, promotions
1,6 -   Good for money and career
1,8 -   Good for money and career
6,8 -   Good for money and fame

Unfavorable Number Combinations:

2,3 -   Arguments, lawsuits and sicknesses
2,5 -   Accidents, deaths
3,7 -   Encounters of robberies and thieves
1,2 -   Divorce and separations

Neutral Number Combinations:

6,7 -   Good for money. Injured by guns.

The Remedies

In general, number combinations which bring about a productive rather than a domination cycle are best. Exercise the correction methods you have learned when a domination cycle exists. However, analysis largely depends on the original nature and symbologies of numbers (see previous page). For example, take the number combination of 2 and 6: 2 (Earth) produces 6 (Metal). This combination generates a productive cycle. With the assistance of 2 (Earth), 6 (Metal), having nature of great wealth, power, and authority is now strengthened. The number 2 (Earth), which stands for sicknesses, pain, and miscarriages, will still prevail. Employing this dual number system for Feng Shui analysis has proven to be highly accurate.

Example 6-6:

A Li House, analyzed in the year 1994.

House Trigram Number = 9 (center quadrant, left side, Normal type)
Annual Number = 6 (center quadrant, right side, *Italic type*)

↑

NW	N	NE

1 *7*	5 *2*	3 *9*
2 *8*	9 *6*	7 *4*
6 *3*	4 *1*	8 *5*

W ... E

SW   S   SE

LLI

Analysis:
1)   East Quadrant — 7, 4
        7 (Metal) dominates (wood).
        This number combination will bring occupants of this quadrant
        injuries or diseases related to the thighs and buttocks, as 4 (Sun
        Trigram) represents these body parts.

2)   North Quadrant — 2, 5
        2 (Earth) and 5 (Earth)
        In Feng Shui, this combination is regarded as the most critical
        and one should avoid using such a quadrant as an entrance or a
        bedroom. The two numbers, although they belong to the same
        element group and do not generate a domination cycle, both
        symbolize sickness and accidents. Great caution should be
        exercised if there are no alternatives but to use such a quadrant
        as either an entrance or a bedroom. Metal reduces Earth, and
        should then be placed in such a quadrant. Any metal ornament
        (except wind chimes) that has moving metal parts and generates
        metallic sounds, such as a grandfather clock, would remedy this
        intensely adverse situation.

3)   South Quadrant — 1, 4
        1 (Water) produces 4 (Wood)
        As mentioned, this combination is best for writing, creativity,
        and fame. The number 4 symbolizes good writing and creativity,
        and is further enhanced by 1, since water nourishes wood.

Feng Shui, aside from helping to find a desirable environment for living
or for work, also fulfills dreams for childless couples who wish for
parenthood, or for individuals who seek harmonious relationships and
companionship. More of this advanced information will appear in the
forthcoming book, *The Xuan Kong System of Feng Shui.*

The following House Trigram and Annual Number combination analysis should be applied in quadrants where the entrances, bedrooms, and home offices are located.

House Tri. No.	Annual No.	Analysis
1	1	Good for academic achievements, artistic creativity. Good for money. Blood, ear, and kidney-related diseases. Accidents caused by alcohol.
1	2	Troubled by spousal relationships. Easily sick and apt to have miscarriages. Involved in car accidents.
1	3	Troubled by gossip, lawsuits, imprisonment, and disasters.
1	4	Good for writing, fame. Also good for new male companionships.
1	5	Easily troubled by sicknesses, food poisonings, and injuries caused by accidents.
1	6	Good for career advancements. Also good for money. Easily troubled by migraine headaches.
1	7	Good for money. Competition at work. Hurt by knives. Easy to bleed.
1	8	Good for money and career advancements. Misunderstandings among siblings or business partners.
1	9	Good for career and money. Eye problems.

House Tri. No.	Annual No.	Analysis
2	1	Troubled by spousal relationships. Easily sick. Miscarriages and car accidents are possible.
2	2	Good for military police, and machine-related work. Easy to get sick, particularly digestive system-related diseases. Injuries by accidents.
2	3	Troubled by gossip, lawsuits, and accidents. Easy to become sick. Particularly harmful to females.
2	4	Good for academic achievements and writing. Malicious sexual encounters for women. Diseases in abdominal region.
2	5	The most critical combination. Stay dormant. Easy to have serious diseases and accidents.
2	6	Good for power and authority. Diseases in abdominal region
2	7	Competition at work. Bleeding. Injury by knives. Easy to fall sick.
2	8	Good for property and money. Easy to fall sick.
2	9	Not good for research and development work. A highly unfavorable combination for children's bedrooms.

House Tri. No.	Annual No.	Analysis
3	1	Troubled by rumors, lawsuits, and imprisonment.
3	2	Easily troubled by rumors, lawsuits and imprisonment. Car accidents are likely. Easy to get sick, particularly for females.
3	3	Easily troubled by fights, quarrels, disagreements, and lawsuits. Easy to encounter robberies.
3	4	Good for writing, academic achievements, and creativity. Malicious sexual encounters.
3	5	Unfavorable for young male adults. Easy to have liver-related and leg-related diseases. Easy to fall sick.
3	6	Good for money. Unfavorable for young men. Leg injuries are likely.
3	7	Easily troubled by quarrels and fights. Encounter robberies. Injured by knives or metal objects.
3	8	Good for money. Unfavorable for children. Injuries in the four limbs.
3	9	Robberies are very likely. Troubled by lawsuits, quarrels, and fights. Fire accidents are likely.

House Tri. No.	Annual No.	Analysis
4	1	Good for academic achievements, artistic creativity, and fame. Good for encountering new male companionship. Extramarital relationships are likely.
4	2	Good for writing. Malicious sexual encounters, for females. Diseases in abdominal region.
4	3	Good for writing and artistic creativity. Malicious sexual encounters are likely.
4	4	Very favorable for writing and artistic creativity. Easy to attract the opposite sex.
4	5	Lack of creativity. Easy to fall sick, particularly to skin diseases.
4	6	Good for money. Unfavorable for writing and creativity. Unfavorable for pregnant women. Thighs and buttocks-related diseases are likely.
4	7	Troubled by quarrels or lawsuits related to inadvertencies in documents. Unfavorable for pregnant women. Thighs- and buttocks-related diseases.
4	8	Good for writing and money. Unfavorable for children. Injuries in the four limbs.
4	9	Good for writing and creativity. Beware of fire accidents.

House Tri. No.	Annual No.	Analysis
5	1	Troubled by diseases, food poisoning, and accidents.
5	2	The most critical number combination. Stay dormant. Serious diseases and deaths are likely.
5	3	Unfavorable for youths. Liver-related or leg-related diseases.
5	4	Lack of creativity. Easy to get sick, especially with skin diseases.
5	5	A very critical combination. Serious diseases and accidents are likely.
5	6	Not good for money. Easy to fall sick. Bones or head region–related diseases.
5	7	Troubled by arguments. Easy to fall sick. Mouth-related diseases.
5	8	Not good for money. Unfavorable for children. Injuries in the four limbs.
5	9	Not good for gambling or buying stocks. Beware of eye diseases. Fire accidents are likely.

House Tri. No.	Annual No.	Analysis
6	1	Good for money and career advancements. Easy to have migraine headaches.
6	2	Good for power and authority. Abdominal region-related diseases.
6	3	Good for money. Unfavorable for youths. Leg injuries.
6	4	Good for money. Unfavorable for writing and creativity. Unfavorable for pregnant women. Thighs and buttocks-related diseases.
6	5	Not good for money. Easy to fall sick. Head-related diseases.
6	6	Very good for money. Injuries caused by metal objects are likely.
6	7	Competition at work. Injuries caused by metal objects during arguments or fights.
6	8	Good for money. Can easily have troubled emotions. Feeling lonely.
6	9	Good for money. Arguments with elders. Head region related diseases.

House Tri. No.	Annual No.	Analysis
7	1	Good for money. Competition at work. Bleeding is likely. Injuries caused by metal objects.
7	2	Competition at work. Bleeding. Easy to fall sick. Injuries by metal objects.
7	3	Troubled by fights and arguments. Robbery is likely. Injuries by metal objects.
7	4	Troubles caused by inadvertencies in documents. Thighs- and buttocks-related diseases. Unfavorable for pregnant women.
7	5	Troubled by arguments and fights. Easy to fall sick. Mouth region-related diseases.
7	6	Good for competitive jobs. Injuries caused by metal objects during arguments or fights.
7	7	Obtain money from competitions. Favorable for young female and entertainment businesses. Beware of bleeding.
7	8	Obtain money from competitions. Favorable for young female and male relationships. Beware of over indulging in sex.
7	9	Good for career advancements and authority. Troubled by fights and arguments. Fire accidents.

House Tri. No.	Annual No.	Analysis
8	1	Good for money and career advancements. Arguments among siblings or business partners.
8	2	Good for properties and money. Easy to fall sick
8	3	Good for money. Unfavorable for children. Injuries in the four limbs.
8	4	Good for writing and creativity. Good for money. Unfavorable for children. Injuries in the four limbs.
8	5	Not good for money. Unfavorable for children. Injuries in the four limbs.
8	6	Good for money. Easily troubled emotions. Feel lonely.
8	7	Obtain money from competitions. Favorable for young female and male relationships. Beware of overindulging in sex.
8	8	Very good for money and properties. Especially good for purchasing properties. A very favorable number combination.
8	9	Good for money and festivities. Arguments between young adults and elders are likely.

House Tri. No.	Annual No.	Analysis
9	1	Good for career advancements and money. Eye-related diseases.
9	2	Not good for research and development work. Unfavorable bedrooms for children.
9	3	Robberies and lawsuits are likely. Beware of fire accidents.
9	4	Good for writing and creativity. Beware of fire accidents.
9	5	Unfavorable for gambling and purchasing stocks. Eye diseases and fire accidents are likely.
9	6	Good for money. Arguments and fights with elders are likely. Head region-related diseases.
9	7	Good for career advancements and authorities. Beware of arguments and fire accidents.
9	8	Good for money and festivities. Arguments and fights between young adults and elders are likely.
9	9	(Assessing this combination requires more information that should be analyzed by a qualified Feng Shui practitioner.)

THE ENVIRONMENT

C
H
A
P
T
E
R

7

THE LIVING ENVIRONMENT

In previous chapters, we have discussed a wide range of effects a house or building has on its occupants. However, we must not overlook the quality of the surrounding area where the building is located. The environment should include the lot size and shape, land elevation, landscape design, etc. These and more are all contributing factors to a desirable environment that will enhance our health, emotions, and wealth.

A popular Chinese proverb (地 靈 人 傑) explains how a good environment or the land on which we live can alter our personalities, attitudes, health and help us excel in many aspects of life.

The following are the introduction to the basics of a desirable environment:

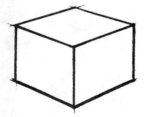 

Figure 7-1

The most desirable shapes for a house or building and its land are squares or slightly rectangular. A building that is desirably shaped needs to have a good flow of Qi, Personal and House Trigrams match, favorable entrance location, and a well-designed interior, in order to be considered a good Feng Shui house.

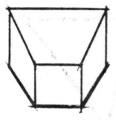 

Figure 7-2

A building with the same length on the two sides, but with a wide facing side and a narrow sitting side, is difficult for retaining wealth. Occupants of such a house will have easily troubled emotions. Therefore, this is considered undesirable.

Figure 7-3

A wide sitting side and a facing side is considered good for retaining wealth, as long as the owner's Personal Trigram matches the House Trigram.

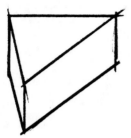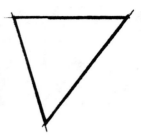

Figure 7-4

A triangular-shaped house, building, or piece of land is considered highly undesirable.

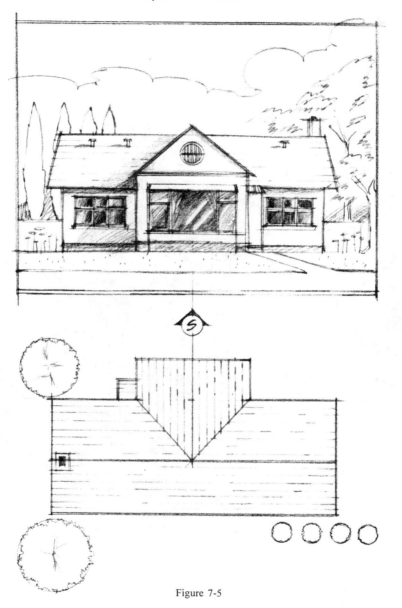

Figure 7-5

A house or building with a protruding southern part, named (龜頭午), is known to have a frequent change of owners.

Figure 7-6

Occupants of a house or building with roads on either side will have sleeping problems and/or mental illness.

Figure 7-7

Houses with roads pointing directly at entrance are not recommended
except for those who acquire in-depth knowledge of Feng Shui. The
effects these types of houses have on occupants can be extreme. It can
bring immense wealth or fatalities.

Figure 7-8

A house with a one-way street along either side of a house's entrance and heading away from the house is considered not good for wealth.

Figure 7-9

A house sitting at the intersection of a Y-shaped road will bring its occupants accidents, robberies, and unproductive careers.

Figure 7-10

A house with a Y-shaped road (or body of water) facing its entrance will bring poverty and reduce productivity to the occupants.

Figure 7-11

A house sitting at the inside curve of a road (or stream of water) with the front side facing the road will bring good wealth, health and career advancements to the occupants.

Figure 7-12

A building with a pitched roof will cause negative effects on the house it faces, particularly if it faces the house's entrance. The negative effects are known as "Sha" (煞), especially when the annual number 2 or 5 resides in the same quadrant as the entrance. Fatalities will occur to the occupants of the house. A sword linked together with coins (Metal) was widely used as a remedy in the past. If a pitched roof faces a Chien quadrant, it will cause problems in the head; when it faces a Li quadrant, it will cause problems in the eyes; when it faces a Kan quadrant, it will cause kidney problems.

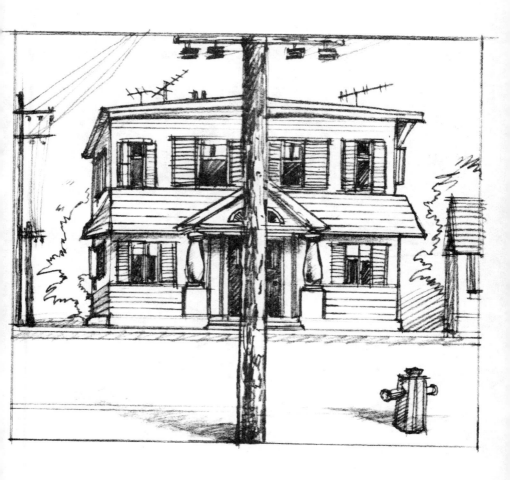

Figure 7-13

Houses with entrances that face south and see high-rise buildings with sharp-pointed ceilings, such as churches or power poles, are considered undesirable. Houses with such environmental Sha will bring fire accidents (南方尖頭多回祿).

Figure 7-14

Unlike the example shown in Figure 7-11, houses sitting on the other side of roads with entrances facing the "blade" are undesirable. This type of house will bring poverty, sickness, and bad luck to the occupants.

Figure 7-15

Avoid living on the same level of (or below) a freeway with the "blade" side facing your residence. This environmental Sha will cause disasters, as well as separations within the families.

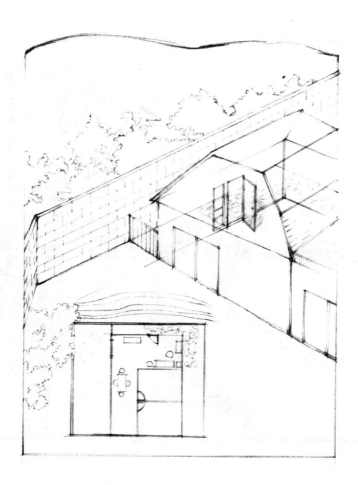

Figure 7-16

Avoid structures whose walls are higher than the house or of the same height. This brings pessimism and poor finances to the occupants of the house. Furthermore, when the house is locked on the people side, the occupant may encounter imprisonment. (This is discussed in more detail in Book III, *The Xuan Kong of Feng Shui*).

Figure 7-17

Avoid structures that are in the proximity of dump sites (environmental Sha). This environment is too unhealthy for anyone to live in.

Figure 7-18

Avoid buildings that are in the proximity of cemeteries and cremation sites. This brings pessimism to the occupants with the exception of nuns, priests, monks and etc.

More on the Environment

The shape of the land on which our houses are built has various influences on us. It can cause imbalances to our bodies and cause personality changes. This is especially true when the location is near an undesirable environment and when the shape of the house is not recommended.

In most cases, a well-experienced Feng Shui practitioner can easily analyze a house with high accuracy. However, there are times that a practitioner may make some discrepancies in judgment. The answer lies in the foundation of the land on which the houses are built.

We need to avoid certain types of land when building houses. This type of environmental Sha overpowers and supersedes other Feng Shui requirements, such as direction, Personal and House Trigram matches, and the Qi. Some examples are:

A)   Burial Sites
      Houses built on land that were once burial sites are considered to be overwhelmingly Yin and will bring uncomfortable feelings to the occupants of the house . Those who know for a fact that they are actually living on land that the dead once occupied, they will then be psychologically troubled.

B)   Slaughter or Execution Sites
      Unsettled spirits usually gather on sites that had a lot of violence and executions. House built on this type of land although designed according to Feng Shui principles, are still considered undesirable.

C)   **Dump Sites**

A landfill is unclean. Hygienically, this type of land is extremely undesirable for anybody. Living in such an environment for a period of time will cause diseases and poor health. The first priority of a good Yang house is a clean and healthy environment where all good Qi is retained.

QUESTIONS & ANSWERS

CHAPTER 8

Questions and Answers

The following questions are often asked in the classes at our Institute.

1) *Which is more important, the Personal Trigram or the House Trigram in the East/West system?*
Both the Personal and House Trigrams share equal importance in the East/West system.

2) *How does a tree positioned at the entrance of a house affect the Feng Shui?*
Any objects as trees or poles that are close to or seem to be blocking the main entrance are bad Feng Shui. The entrance serves as the main opening for the inflow of Qi.

3) *I have heard that houses with roads pointing directly at the entrances will bring grave effects to the occupants of the house. Is this true?*
Houses with roads pointing directly at the main entrances are considered unfavorable. The effects can be intense and extreme.

4) *From the Xuan Kong teaching, I found out that I have a 1 and a 9 combination in my bedroom. Do you think the wood furniture in the bedroom will automatically help to remedy the domination?*
Number 1 (Kan) stands for the water element. Number 9 (Li) stands for the fire element. Yes, a remedy is needed for the dominance that water has over fire. The answer to this domination is wood; however, wood furniture is dead wood. Strong, green stalks of plants properly represent the wood element. You may want to substitute plants with the color green.

5) *I have often seen people using mirrors as a remedy for bad Qi in a house. How does it work?*

The remedy we use for any kind of domination that exist in our homes remain within the Five Elements. Mirrors do not belong to any of these elements. Mirror in our day- to- day lives are only for reflection. They can only reflect light rays but not Qi. In the past, Chinese used polished brass to reflect one's image. Those would be the only kind of mirrors that can be used as a metal element remedy in Feng Shui. Octagonally shaped mirrors, often known by the general public as Ba Gua mirrors, serve as no remedy in Feng Shui.

6) *Do windchimes play a part in Feng Shui?*

Yes, they do. Only wind chimes made of metal are considered as the metal remedy for earth domination over water, or when you see a critical number such as 2. However, there are times when using windchimes can be dangerous. This will be further discussed in our advanced material in Book III.

7) *We have been taught to use the actual substance of the Five Elements for remedies. Then what about a fire element remedy? I cannot build a fire in my bedroom all year long.*

You may use lamps with red shades which strengthen the fire element. You may also use an electric heater in the winter, as electricity is also considered a fire element. These suggestions stand for the fire element.

8) *Can I use a western compass instead of a Lo Pan?*

Yes, a western compass that gives an accurate directional reading is an alternative to our Lo Pan.

9) *Is Feng Shui related to Buddhism?*

No. Feng Shui is not related to any kind of religion. All principles and theories of Feng Shui are derived from the Yi-Jing, the Book of Change.

10) *How often do you tell people to move from their houses after you have done a reading?*

This happens very rarely. Remedies often solve the adversities. When there are the critical number combinations at the entrance or when the environment is overwhelmingly bad and no remedy can cure the situation, only then we suggest that the occupants move out of the house.

11) *My wife and I belong to different groups. Can Feng Shui help the problems in our marriage?*

Always remember Feng Shui helps us to identify and manipulate the Qi. in our environment. By doing so, we have the power to maximize the potential of our homes and minimize the adversities. Feng Shui is a natural science for living comfort; it is not astrology. In fact, in many ways Feng Shui can help couples to bridge their miscommunication by selecting appropriate directions, a suitable bedroom, and a house that is good for relationships.

12) *How many fish do I need to put in my aquarium in order to make it work as the water element remedy?*

You need only water when there is a domination between the elements of metal and wood. Clean and moving water will do the job. The fish only serve to beautify the aquarium.

13) *Does Feng Shui apply only to houses?*

Feng Shui can apply to the city you live in, the state, and even the world. It helps each of us pick the right direction for our personal advancements.

14) *My friends have been asking me what school of Feng Shui am I learning?*

You may call the East/West system a school and Xuan Kong as another. In fact, both of them belong to one school: the school of Feng Shui. Each system represents a different level in Feng Shui. Combining both systems with the environment and applying the Five Elements theories will help to give you the most accurate solutions to your living environment. Always remember Feng Shui is derived from the Yi-Jing and there is only one type of Feng Shui.

15) *I live in a two-story townhouse. How do the two systems apply to the second story of the house?*

The two systems apply to a multi-story house the same as a single-story house. More on this and other structures, such as apartments, commercial buildings, etc., will be discussed in Book II and Book III of our Feng Shui series.

Return Policies

Warranty:
Sang's Lo Pan is under a 30-day warranty.

Exchanges:
Lo Pans with defective parts may be returned within the warranty period in exchange for a replacement. Please return it in our original box with our packing slip or invoice, stating your reason of return to:

Returns Dept.
The American Feng Shui Institute
108 North Ynez Avenue, #202
Monterey Park, CA 91754

Please allow a replacement two weeks after receipt of your returned unit.

Refunds:
Non-defective (in good and reasonable condition) Lo Pans that are returned for refunds and are within the warranty period are entitled to a full refund (delivery charges are not refundable). Please allow a four-week period for check payments, and two billing cycles for credit card payments.

There will be a 15% restocking charge for Lo Pans that are returned for refunds and after expiration of warranty (delivery charges are not refundable). Please allow a four-week period for check payments, and two billing cycles for credit card payments.

Sang's Lo Pan Order Form

(Please Print)
Name: _____

Address: _____

_____

_____

Tel (Home): _____

Tel (Work): _____

Lo Pan @ US$50.00 each
Please send check or money order to :
The American Feng Shui Institute.
108 North Ynez Avenue, Ste. #202
Monterey Park, California 91754

Quantity

☐ x US$50.00 .... US $_____

Freight Charges (in US only) .... US $ 3.80

Sales Tax (8.25% for delivery to CA) ___ US $_____

Total: US $_____

Payment Method: Please do not send cash. No CODs.

☐ I've enclosed a check or money order in U.S. funds. Checks must have your name preprinted on them. Returned checks are subject to a service charge for the greater of $15 or maximum amount allowed by state law.

☐ Visa   ☐ MasterCard

Card No. _____

Expiration Date _____

Print Name _____

Signature _____

☐ Yes, I want to be put on your mailing list for your updated book list.
Please see Return Policy and Product Warranty on back of Order Form.

Application Form

(Please Print)

Name: _____

Address: _____

_____

_____

Tel. (Home) : _____

Tel (Work) : _____

Date of Birth: _____

Social Security Number: _____

Name of Employer: _____

Occupation: _____

Educational Background (Degree and Institutions)

_____   _____

_____   _____

_____   _____

Course: Feng Shui/Beginning Class - Section 1
Amount $195
(One Day/7 Hour course)

Payment Method: Please do not send cash. Send all payments to: The American Feng Shui Institute, 108 North Ynez Avenue, #202, Monterey Park, California 91754

☐ I've enclosed a check or money order in U.S. funds. Checks must have my name preprinted on them. I understand that returned checks are subject to a service charge for the greater of $15 or maximum amount by the state law.

☐ Visa   ☐ MasterCard

Card No. _____

Expiration Date _____

Print Name _____

Signature _____

☐ Yes, I want to be put on your mailing list for your updated book list.

* Please note that there will be no refunds on cancellations one day prior to class.